ERANOS 1996

JOURNAL

ERANOS 1996

JARBUCH - YEARBOOK - ANNALES

VOLUME 65

Presentations of the 1995 Eranos/Uehiro
Round Table Session
Ascona, Switzerland
May, 1995

THE ERANOS FOUNDATION
THE UEHIRO FOUNDATION

THE SHADOW OF PERFECTION

PAPERS PRESENTED AT THE 1995 ROUND TABLE SESSION

EDITORS

JAMES G. DONAT AND JAY LIVERNOIS

SPONSORED BY

THE ERANOS FOUNDATION

THE UEHIRO FOUNDATION ON ETHICS AND EDUCATION

SPRING JOURNAL, INC.

THE ERANOS ROUND TABLE SESSIONS

The Round Table Sessions, which include formal lectures, group discussions, and individual work with the *I Ching's* texts, are open to the public upon previous registration. For more information write to: The Eranos Foundation, Via Moscia 127, CH-6612 Ascona, Switzerland.

Printed in the United States of America
Spring Journal Edition ISBN 1-882670-08-6
Eranos Edition ISBN 3-9520054-7-9

CONTENTS

This volume should be quoted as

ERANOS 65-1996.

CHRISTA ROBINSON

OPENING WORDS AT THE SECOND JOINT ERANOS AND UEHIRO ROUND TABLE SESSION, MAY 1995

I am happy to welcome you here to Eranos. It is my particular pleasure to greet our Japanese friends from the Uehiro Foundation on Ethics and Education. We are grateful to Mr. Eiji Uehiro for his generous and open-minded cooperation with Eranos in the sessions on "The Ethic of the Image."

You have come to this meeting place, travelling from the different parts of the world, each moved by personal expectations and imaginings. But the common aim is to extend and deepen our understanding of the human propensity for perfection and the shadows that propensity casts. The speakers will attempt to analyze different aspects of the dark side of this ambition and the absolute. At the round table we will compare our experiences with the material presented by the speakers.

In nature we perceive that the shadows cast by the sun are a harmonious play of contrasts. Yet this graded observation is sorely lacking when it comes to imagining the Absolute Good. For citizens of industrialized countries, being buried in the avalanche of modern computers, laser, and communication technology, has only enhanced our craving to concretize our highest ideals, and inclined us to ignore the realities of everyday living. Seemingly without connection to this aspiration for a perfect life in a perfect world, an extremely dark scenery has also emerged—the horrors of the illegal drug business, the tragic bombings by religious and political fanatics, the latest criminal phenomenon of terrorism "for sale," and an ever-growing nihilistic "no-future" mood among the younger generations all over the world.

The awareness of this dangerous and threatening discrepancy has constellated the topic of this Session. Both the light aspects of the striving for "the ideal" and the shadow sides in individual and social life are conspicuously juxtaposed. The dramatic split of light and dark obliges us to be aware, to examine the interplay of light and shadow as nature shows us in its daily and annual rhythms.

This dramatic split throughout the world and on all levels of existence calls for a renewal of the sense of responsibility for each individual. Our work with the *I Ching* as a tool for gaining specific ethical attitudes focuses upon the interplay between the light and dark sides of our lives.

The lectures presented here will be trails that we can follow to see how the shadows of out "light" ambitions affect us; where we meet them in the inside and outside world; and how they present themselves differently in the East and West.

I would also like to express my deep gratitude to Mr. Noboru Maruyama for his ever-competent and relentless cooperation in our common striving for a new ethic. It is with joy and interest that I am looking forward to the next few days.

EIJI UEHIRO

THE PRACTICAL ETHICS ASSOCIATION AND THE
UEHIRO FOUNDATION ON ETHICS AND EDUCATION

Man's wish to "Live a More Virtuous Life" is reflected in numerous religions. However in Japan there has been a tendency for "New Religion" groups to tie the above quest for virtue in with their emphasis on tailoring people's daily lives to their word's actions, and heart. They teach that people's feelings of "Hate," "Anger," or "Desire" should be discarded as "Dust"; and that devoting oneself to one's "Chosen Work" is the true faith. The metaphor "Dusting Off" is an appropriate description of how human beings address the question of "Shadows" in their lives, and how they deal with them. But this poses a problem. Since such solutions are based on the teaching of a particular religion, unless one believes in the "God" of that religion, this attractive educational result cannot be attained.

Among the groups established to promote educational activities (without adherence to any particular God) and direct the course of people's hearts in their daily lives is the Practical Ethics Association, or Empirical Ethics and Fairness Group, funded through the Uehiro Foundation. The Practical Ethics Association, which has much in common with the *Kokoro no Tetsugaku*, or "Philosophy of the Heart," came into being during the pre-modern Edo period, and its activities have spanned the half-century since the end of World War II as Japan's largest and most influential educational organization dealing with ethics.

In the Practical Ethics Association, "Ethics" is the standard by which people decide their daily lives, and people are encouraged to reason and to live according to the ways of "Mother Nature." The "Ethics" and "Mother Nature" we speak of here do not exist as a "Standard" to restrict people's thoughts and actions as an external force. Rather it is something that is pulled out from within those who wish to "Live More Ethically," and is something that is within us all. Born of one's own intent and volition, it comes about through an interaction between one's emotions and the human will to "Seek Virtue."

Based on the above idea, the group's members are instructed in various mental attitudes to prepare for the challenges of living their daily lives. People are taught not to take the phenomena of daily life superficially. One must consider the meaning behind each occurrence as it is encountered.

For example, the members learn that in interpersonal relationships, one's feelings towards another are reflected back onto oneself. In other words, if you feel that someone holds feelings of animosity towards you, the reason is not due to what is within the other person's heart, rather the cause is within you and how you feel animosity towards that person. And by according the other party the utmost in goodwill, it has been demonstrated that such relationships can improve.

There is an expression, "A Child Mirrors His Parent." By learning that children's behavior owes much to the life attitudes of their parents, people can be more reflective of their own life-styles, instead of blaming their children when problems occur.

There is another expression, "Suffering is the Red Light of Life." If one is suffering, there are aspects of one's life that require modification. The "Red Light" is a warning. As also expressed in the words, "Pain and Suffering are the Gates to Happiness," one can change and better one's own situation and circumstances.

In order that people make the above ideas their own, and in order to polish their attitudes of acceptance, the Practical Ethics Association holds daily morning seminars at more than 600 locations, all beginning at 5 A.M. At these seminars, the members recite the "Morning Pledge," consisting of five items relating to effective living, and also listen to the Chairman's message. Then for forty-five minutes, they share their personal experiences. Through the sharing of ideas pertaining to the acceptance of the daily occurrences in their lives, and how each was able to better his or her life attitudes, the participants remember what they may have forgotten about such perspectives, or learn about views of life they may not have considered before. At times, they are offered advice from an experienced group leader, but central is the "Mutual Study" conducted among the participants themselves.

Unlike divination, which has a concrete symbol, the attempt here is to treat the daily events of one's life as a symbol of "Mother Nature" itself, and to accept them through learned "Habit." The members think of all events and occurrences, no matter how insignificant, as a "Signal from Mother Nature," enabling them to be introspective and reflective on their own lives. By such means it is possible to bring out the "Goodness" that is within us all.

"There is No Graduation from This Study," and there are no established goals in this type of introspection and self-betterment. This quest for "Ethics" and "Reason According to Mother Nature" involves a dynamic spirit. And by living in this way, people are able to gain endless fulfillment in their daily lives.

Currently, in Japan, there is much talk about the alleged involvement of a religious group in the poison gas attack in the subway system. This group is considered a newer religion than the previous mentioned, such that scholars label it "New-New Religion." My own feeling is that no matter how different it may seem, its members wish to "Live a More Virtuous Life." The problem being that they have formed a group that segregates itself from the outside world and stands in denial of the reality of life as it exists in society.

In divination, which originated in China, we are offered a compass by which to direct our lives for the better. And, here at Eranos, also notice the penetrating insights into synchronicity pointed out by Jung and its applicability to the real lives of people. In Japan, too, we find similarities to the principle of "Empirical Ethics." When people are trying to live more virtuously, it becomes important how we deal with the "Shadow" that lurks in the unconscious. Wherewith I sincerely hope that through this conference, we will be able to add a new page to the efforts mankind had made since prehistoric times.

CLAUDIO BONVECCHIO

THE PERFECT KINGDOM

1. The Perfect Kingdom

A voice—at the rise of the Christian era—stands high and strong. It belongs to Augustine (354-430 C.E.), the great Doctor of the Church. His words, as heavy as boulders, hit the kingdoms of "this world." *"Remota itaque iustitia,"* says Augustine, *"quid sunt regna nisi magna latrocinia? Quia et latrocinia quid sunt nisi parva regna?"*[1] The judgment is severe. The sentence—based on the words *magna-parva*, is unappealable. The powers of the world come out destroyed. They are the receptacles of each degradation; they are the hideout of each scoundrel. A condition which: *"remota sit iustitia."*

Of course, Augustine, with the ability of a worn-out rhetorician does not consider that the *"remota iustitia"* may be an irreversible destiny.[2] He keeps alive, though faint, the hope—or the dream—that, on earth, the kingdom of justice might establish itself. In that case, the kingdom is no longer the den of thieves and pirates to which, eleven centuries later, Bodin refers.[3] Instead, it is the earth, blissful and perfect, where justice rules, undisputed, and with it, peace, tranquillity, and serenity.

Within Augustine grows the hypothesis of an encounter between the two cities, otherwise divided: earthly Jerusalem and heavenly Jerusalem. Lord and sovereign of it, in first place, is Christ, creator of the world (*Pantokrator*); and in second place, is the perfect king who must be his mirror.[4]

In the Augustinian eventuality of a "totally other" and a "totally right" world, hides the ancestral hope of turning into positive what man experiences in life as negative. It is the vision of a perfect world which mankind would want as its world: real and concrete. Therein prefigures the desire, in the depths of the spirit, of a radical metabasis, of a new disposition of the soul. It sends one to an idyllic *aestas aurea*, dramatically lost and eternally yearned for. "They, looking back, all th' eastern side beheld/Of Paradise, so late their happy seat...."[5] These are the verses of John Milton's (1608-1674) *Paradise Lost*; they give us poetic voice to this burning, yearning desire.[6]

But the *aurea aetas* is nothing but the symbolic dimension in which mankind projects—as Eliade and van der Leeuw notice—the nostalgia for the origins, to which he longs to go back and find again a lost fullness.[7] From the *Admonition* of the Egyptian feudal age,[8] to Homer,[9] to Hesiod (8th? century B.C.E.),[10] Virgil's (70-19 B.C.E.) *Bucolics*[11]—just to mention some of the greatest—there is a constant call to a joyful past which leads to an aching remembrance and an anxious wait.

Nostalgia often interlaces with the anxiety of the *reditus* and with the certainty of remaining, eternally, in the original status. It is the redemption from this world; promised in the words of Christ to the suffering thief on the cross: "Verily I say unto thee, To day shalt thou be with me in Paradise";[12] and trustfully echoed in the second Sura of the *Koran*: "But, bear the glad tidings to those who believe and work righteousness, that for them are gardens beneath which rivers flow; whenever they are provided with fruit therefrom they say, 'This is what we were provided with before....'"[13] They are tokens of the return of salvation, both human and divine. Thus Paradise shows itself as the Perfect Kingdom, revealed by the prophets and chanted by the poets. Here the lamb grazes with the wolf; nature produces abundant harvests; milk and honey flow in the fountains; inequality, injustice, and death are banned altogether.[14]

It shows itself as the exact opposite of the world in which mankind historically lives.[15] According to Efrem the Syrian (c. 306-373C.E.), Paradise is situated in the antichthonic place; the place opposing the inhabited earth, told by Aristotle (384-322 B.C.E.) and Eratosthenes of Cyrene (c. 275-194 B.C.E.).[16] Paradise is the kingdom of joy, opposed to the one of sorrow. It is the magnificent seat of the blessed, described—in the whole of its splendor—in John's *Apocalypse*.[17]

In this Eden-like and Paradisiacal earth,[18] the elements of the passage are highly symbolic. They are the symbols which go back to totality and transcendency: the mountain, the tree, the water, the light.[19] They are the expressions of the *unio mistica* which grips the sky and earth in a *hieros gamos* (sacred marriage), in turn, a perfect materialization of the *Unus Mundus*.[20] The world which, according to the famous alchemist Dorneus, is the potential world of the first day of creation, the world of the perfect union of each contrary.[21] The power which unfolds in itself, is the numinus force which moves and pervades Creation. Dante (1265-1321) calls it, "eternal light, existing in yourself alone, / Alone knowing yourself; and who, known to yourself / And knowing, Love and smile upon yourself."[22]

It is the Sacred *Eros* of the ancients which feeds life and which turns death into a bloodless and painless fusion with the whole. A whole which represents for the human who is part of it, the abyss of Oneself, or like the experience of the divine. This is why the nudity which is its mark is, for the mystic Johann Tauler (1300-1361), the participation in the "divine abyssal", it communicates the auroral and primitive freedom of existence.[23]

Such freedom marks, gnostically, the distance from each law and constriction. As the original kingdom, it is a kingdom *of* this world, but it is not *in* this world. It shows itself in the purity and in the full syntony with the One that Goethe (1749-1832) calls *"wirkende Natur"* (living natural).[24] A Nature which is a benign and protective mother, not terrible and hostile.

The age of symbology which unfolds, reveals the mythical imprint of this "imaginal earth."[25] Such a symbology is present in the Sumerian myths,[26] in the *Gilgamesh saga,*[27] in the architectonic gardens of Persia and Moghul India,[28] in the transfigurant splendor of Siddhartha's last home,[29] in the stories of Cacuntala from the *Mahabharata,*[30] or in the Asgard of Nordic Edda novels.[31] The point of conversion between space and time[32] are both surmounted in a superior vision, where psychic melts with pneumatic, where material melts with spiritual, and vice versa. Its position is at the East, where the sun rises and where everything begins.[33]

In the land where fatigue is unknown, and where death does not outrage life, peace and harmony spring out from spontaneity, not from a law or coercion. This blissful condition is mentioned by Plato (429?-347 B.C.E.), in the *Politics,* with a veiled nostalgia. The reminiscence goes back to the time in which Kronos reigns, when no government and no masters have control over mankind, but where everything flows continually and abundantly from Nature's fertile breast.[34]

In tight symbiosis with Creation, man's life unravels averse from each pain, from each tension, from each mourning. Blissfulness here, is one with happiness and with eternal spring. Pindar (518?-438 B.C.E.) makes it the home of the ones who have travelled unhurt through tests and reincarnation, thus deserving the epithet of "just men." He calls them "Lucky Islands", associating the *status aureus* (golden condition) of Nature, justice, rectitude, to joy, well being and remuneration.[35] On the contrary, the common world, the world of daily living—the Christian *saeculum* (age)—carries the stigmata of pain, of sorrow, of desperation. All the elements which identify the kingdom of perfection and which make of it an intersection between macrocosm and microcosm, are present.[36]

Situated at the extreme point of the aqueous world, beyond the Ocean—as Hesiod wants it[37]—or maybe at its center,[38] the Perfect Kingdom or Paradisiacal kingdom, shows itself as an island, or as a *hortus conclusus* (circumscribed garden). The etymology of the word "Paradise" comes from the Persian *pairi* (around) and *daeza* (wall).[39] It is, indeed, a circumscribed territory, whose circumference is imprecise and whose access is protected by a curtain of flames, or by a circle of crystal or emerald stones, or precious metals;[40] where the trees which grow are unusual and healthy,[41] while the miraculous waters herald eternal youth.[42] Only just men can enter it, or exceptionally, some men particularly bold and courageous.[43]

The Christian world, after a first and justifiable wariness, does not move away from the mystic tale. Instead, it moves it into its own doctrinal tradition, assimilating it and enriching it symbolically, and tries to push it towards the aims of an intransigent and theological system.[44] However, despite each caution, the poetic word tends to overlap the prophetic one, and the great Latin and Greek *auctores* (authors) are engaged as a confirmation of the Biblical steps and in anticipation of the evangelical ones. The testimonies of Justin Martyr (100-165 C.E.),

Tertullian (100-225 C.E.), Lactantius (240-320 C.E.) are authoritative proof.[45] With the *Esamerone* by Basil of Caesarea (330-379 C.E.)—and especially with the *Pseudo-Basil* (a text from the 3rd century C.E.)—the creation of *Genesis*—the complete and perfect world of the origins—assumes the tone, the color, and the *pathos* of the pagan *aetas aurea* (golden age).[46]

The earthly Paradise confuses itself with the "Lucky Islands," adding to the severity of the theological, the awesomeness of the marvellous. In this magic *koine* (mixture), where the power of the Sacred seems to prevail, a double danger is outlined. On the one hand, the human and moral value of the pagan beliefs asserts itself to the detriment of the doctrinarian purity of Christianity; on the other, the mythological and symbolic aspects of paganism, so scornfully judged by the Fathers of the Church as fantasies of a demoniacal nature, acquires religious credibility.

There is a hybrid mixture which amalgamates realism and fantasy, Sacred and Mythological, earthly desires and unearthly truths. The Perfect Kingdom, Paradise—assimilated to the Lucky Islands—shows itself as a symbolic aim, but geographically reachable. The traveller's curiosity, the boldness of the adventurer, and the anxiety of the explorer seem to level out with the virtues of the devoted or of the intrepid who dares to measure himself with the tough tests of the spirit.[47]

Against such a possibility and devious danger, the supporters of an allegoric and mystic reading of Paradise line up, though indirectly and cautiously;[48] and, with them, the ones like Isidore of Seville (560-636 C.E.), who prefer to be at a distance from questionable combinations and overlappings.[49] But precautions and attentions are worthless. Beyond polemic and doubt, a syncretistic reading asserts itself, where the earthly elements mix with the unearthly ones. They consolidate in spite of each allegoric and figurated interpretation, a realistic vision with a strong tone. It is Augustine who is the great *patron* (maker) of this operation.

With his unquestioned and unquestionable authority, Augustine confirms the existence of what the Sacred texts say about the Perfect Kingdom Paradise. "These proofs," he states, " should persuade us to take in the literal way the other details, and see in them not a figurative way of speaking. They are not only real facts, narrated as historical, but also figures of another reality."[50] In the furrow of his authoritative opinion, the entire medieval culture, from Rabanus Maurus (776 or 784-856 C.E.) to Peter Lombard (1100-1160 C.E.),[51] accredits to him the earthly reality of Paradise, even highlighting, as Thomas Aquinas (1225-1274 C.E.) did, its character of *locus spiritualis* (spiritual territory).[52] It is a neatly prefigured conclusion, both in the primitive draft of the 9th and 10th centuries, and in the latest popularization from the 12th century onwards of the medieval best-seller, *Navigatio Sancti Brendani.*[53]

Of this double record, both material and spiritual, the image of the paradisiacal kingdom settles down definitely. Its perdurability is secular. It extends uncontested until the encounter of the truth of faith with the truth of reason, ending with the advantage of the latter.[54]

The Perfect Kingdom, the paradisiac kingdom, loses the enamel of wonder and the redeeming seduction of the Sacred. Voltaire (1694-1778) does not consider it an imprecise reproduction of the Arabian gardens,[55] and the French encyclopedists consider it a "change of state."[56] The former translated it into the language of secularized natural science, and the latter into the behavioral dictates of bourgeois *"honnete homme."*[57] Little seems to remain of the old fascination.

A trace remains, vaguely covered with exoticism, in Rousseau's (1712-1778) discovery of the state of nature,[58] or in philosophical backgrounds in which Kant (1724-1804) inscribes the rational progress of man. "Reason," he writes, "shows him Paradise as the first stay of his species; but the exit from this Paradise is nothing but his passage from the state of savageness to the state of humanity...from the protection of nature to the state of freedom."[59]

Any reading of Paradise which may not be exclusively symbolic becomes unprovable, while faith in its spiritual existence becomes even more problematical, until it is subsumed as a literary metaphor. In a completely secularized society, it can do nothing but occupy the borderline spaces of a perceptively dilated sensibility: on the one side pathological; on the other, ecstatic.

In this picture, Pardise, the Perfect Kingdom of the "Lucky Islands," is not the mystic place in which justice governs, as in the *aetas aurea* (golden age) so dear to Augustine. It is not even the impossible aim of adventurous journeys or insatiable curiosity. It is however the possibility of an imaginary trip, which keeps its aura intact and fascinating. It is the personal and collective trip, interior and exterior, towards the extreme boundaries of action and thinking, towards the center which is the real hereafter of each philosophical limit.

The image of Paradise is proven by its usual recurrence, in daily language and political ideology. The image is a synonym of a feasible and concrete aim, that human progress should reach, and which is also a synonym of the certainty of new life.[60] It coincides with the positive epilogue of the history, or of one history, with a tension towards the totality of the origin—towards the *Unus Mundus*. And, with the conviction that in the imperfect hieroglyphics of human behavior, there hides a concealed perfection, a secret order. Both perfection and order are the magic phonemes which hold and disclose Paradise. Like a Dantean Ulysses and his journey's companions of journey,[61] one may dare to penetrate into Paradise, to discover and understand, confiding in Saint Brendan's fate, and not that of Ulysses.

2. The Perfect Kingdom and the Collective Unconscious

Setting aside the most famous learned and literary narrations, we pause over the Paradisiacal descriptions of the Perfect Kingdom found in the less famous expressions of the Collective Unconscious. Wherein lies a pacific coexistence between Christian-theological elaboration and legendary-pagan elements.[62] Which proves the existence—in the image of the Perfect Kingdom—of a common basis spontaneously evoked.

Let us now consider two popular and legendary frescos. The one referring to the land of Cockaigne, or the land of plenty, and the other to the kingdom of Prester John. Their fame is surprising, their diffusion extraordinary, and the particularity of their contents such as to give life to an iconographic genre. Many of their themes, secularized and idealologized, appear in the modern substitute for the Perfect Kingdom: utopias.

The first, the land or kingdom of Cockaigne,[63] has a famous antecedent in the "Isle of the Blissful" described in Book II of the *True Story*

of Lucian of Samosata (c. 120-200 C.E.).[64] A land wherein Lucian describes not the usual climatic mildness, pleasantness of places, and
happiness, instead, the abundance of products—both necessary and
unnecessary.[65] The exceptional fertility of the Nature, here, joins with
the independent creativity of man's work. So, the earth, together with
its fruits, produces what man's senses desire: ointments, bread, etc. But
the rivers of wine, the fountains of honey, vines which give milk, the
trees whose branches are full of glasses of wine, are nothing but the
display of libidinal energy and its power. The incredible and atypical,
joined together with the normal and typical, show—visualized by the
imaginary lens—its prodigious force and power. The coronation of it is
in the sexual freedom which improves,[66] as in the Islamic Paradise,[67] a
sort of spiritualized kingdom of Cockaigne—the fan of material pleasure.

In the *Li fabliaus de Coquaigne*, a text from the 13th century and a
model of its genre,[68] and later in Boccaccio's (1313-1375) *Decameron*,[69]
these components are summarized and amplified. They are also repro-
posed in later works of similar contents.[70] There are eternal laid tables,
houses of bread, sausage and cheese, rivers of milk and wine, quadru-
plicated festivities, money in great abundance, sexual recklessness and
eternal youth for everyone.

It would be diverting and restrictive to also attribute to this place of
abundance, the description of a poor, hungry world, tormented by death
and suffering,[71] or to make simple and illusory products of excited and
gastric fantasies. It is, instead, an effective figuration of totality, picked
in its vital, nutritive and generative properties. It is the spontaneous
materialization of the libidinal energy in a motherly and uroboric[72] primordial figure. A magnanimous mother, provident and rescuing, which
clasps the children, needy and suffering, in a consoling and medical
archetypal hug.[73]

Mother Nature is the perennial and overabundant, productive and
reproductive, fountain from which the "water of life" should be drawn—
the hidden treasure of the unconscious. It is the certainty that the
man-son will never be abandoned. Indeed, that he can freely use whatever she offers him as an eternal refuge and comfort from daily threats.
Of course recurrence to the motherly archetype, because of the direct

contact with the libidinal energy of the Collective Unconscious, puts into action certain infractive spurs, anti-authoritative and orgiastic.

This is why the kingdom of Cockaigne is *no kingdom*.[74] In a famous painting by Pieter Brueghel the Elder (1525?-1569), *The Land of Cockaigne*, soldiers, peasants, literates are portrayed without any social differentiation.[75] One understands why both pauperism and heretical movements in medieval times,[76] and anarchical, socialistic, and communistic utopias in modern times,[77] draw from the archetype of the mother—faith and hope for an individual, and a collective new life in a different and just destiny for humankind.

The motherly archetype denotes the existence of a compensatory necessity, against the spiritual and against man's authoritarian excess. This is the case in the medieval age, when the spiritual-celestial-fatherly archetype is impending and overwhelming, both in the social-political way and in the conscious-unconscious sphere of the individual. So, against the risk of an excessive spiritualization, the unconscious confirms the equal importance of the earth, mother and Goddess.[78] And as a motherly archetype, it presents itself both as eternally young and the donor of eternal youth. Whoever washes in its waters—the fountain of youth is the real center of the kingdom of Cockaigne—can enjoy eternal life. From the earth, not only from the sky, comes salvation. So the *Tabla Smaragdina* wisely says, *"Omne superius sicut inferius"* (everything is superior and inferior as well).

The second is the kingdom of Prester John. One may consider it as completing-perfecting the land of Cockaigne. *"Presbiter Iohannes, potentia at virtute Dei et domini nostri Iesu Christi dominus dominatium..."* This is the *incipit* of the famous letter, sent by Prester John to the Emperor of Byzantium, Michael Comnenus, and destined to give life to a long and elaborate legend.[79] Few have considered its veridicality and its presumptuous and historical antecedents, and few people have considered its hypothetical geographic situation, the secret message it carries or the political-literary hermeneutics which may be drawn from it.

Wonder is provoked by the aura of totality which it gives out, and the symbolic richness which it unfolds. Both make one think that we are in front of an image from the deep, spontaneously generated, like a dream or a fantasy. The characters in Prester John's kingdom may be drawn closer, by analogy, to the ones in the Collective Unconscious.

Situated, like the Collective Unconscious, in a magic region, mysterious and other (India),[80] it manifests itself as a *complexio oppositorum*. It extends from East to West, each living being resides there, real and oneiric,[81] Christian and pagan. The great abundance of precious stones— emeralds, topazes, amethysts, onyxes, rubies, etc.—which may be found there and that adorn the palace, weapons and furnishings,[82] is connected symbolically, to the productivity and splendor of Nature. But it is connected, especially, to the secret and suggestive harmony between the quality of the minerals and their psychic virtues, something already coded in the ancient Greek lapidaries.[83] The extreme fertility of the earth, the climatic mildness, the absence of work, the manna which in great abundance falls from Heaven,[84] reminds us of the motherly archetype of the Collective Unconscious, found in the land of Cockaigne.

The Collective Unconscious, in the kingdom of Prester John, is to be found in the fountains of eternal youth[85] and in the caverns inhabited by dragons, tamed, domesticated and trained.[86] They are symbols of great importance and an index of an alchemy from the deep. The fountain, in fact, may be connected to the *aqua permanens* which, for the alchemists "is the wisdom or the knowledge," the "truth" or the "spirit." Its source is hidden in the interior man.[87] Such water is, according to Jung, "an omnipresent substance which pervades everything, an *anima mundi*…and at the same time the supreme treasure *(maximus thesaurus)*, the most hidden and secret numinous reality."[88] This is confirmed in Prester John's letter, where it speaks of a concave boulder containing a miraculous water of curing power.[89] The immediate connection is to the *lapis philosophorum*, the stone of perfection, the sublimate uroboric, the perfection of the Self.[90]

Then again, the symbol of the *uroboric* (the snake which bites its own tail) connects itself to the inhabitant of the cavern, the dragon. It is, "from the psychological point of view…a personification of the instinctual soul"[91] which has to be won and tamed to be able to produce, in the union with conscience, the redeeming transformation of the *complexio oppositorum*. This is why Jung mentions the equivalence between the dragon, the priest, and Christ: the redeemer by name.[92]

The fountain of youth and the dragon can be considered as symbols of the Collective Unconscious, as *sapientia mundi*, as a force eternally existent, in eternal change, but at the same time in perfect equilibrium.

It is the unconscious which, as a totality, fills in the motherly aspect which is so heavily present in the kingdom of Cockaigne.

It is proven by the sensuality and sexual freedom—characterizing a hermaphroditic-uroboric phase of the Collective Unconscious; and by the individual unconscious,[93] which, in the kingdom of Prester John, rises to a higher and equilibrated synthesis. Prester John says, "Among us there is no adulterousness. No vice has power amongst us."[94]

One should pause over the figure which represents this perfect world; Prester John himself. Sovereign and priest, he reigns pacifically, a sump-tuous palace which reminds us of the fabulous one, of the wise king Solomon. A prodigious mirror helps him govern, by enabling him to see whatever is planned to his advantage or disadvantage. The mirror is at the top of a double pyramid, formed, starting from the two bases—superior and inferior—by eight pedestals and sixty-four columns.[95] Such a complicated architectonic structure reminds us of the gnositc *ogdoade*, numerically wise and symbolically wise. As a totality of the *pleroma*,[96] it is considered by Jung as identical to the unconscious.[97] The mirror re-inforces this image, as a symbol of the Self, therefore a synthesis of the subjective and objective. "So Christ, or the Self, is a mirror."[98]

Prester John is the archetypal figure of totality and perfection. Some distinctive signs relate him to heroic and regal characters of the *Grail* saga. In the old French version of *The Letter of Prester John*, the just king and heroic knight are found, as typologies akin to Arthur.[99] And the modest name of priest is proof of the greatness of the wise and the virtue of the just.[100] Such humbleness encloses, like a precious box, per-fection. The one, to imitate Christ-Self, which man and humankind must exercise if they want to rise to the *Great Opera* and be transfigured in the *Filius solis*, to participate in the fullness of the unconscious, and in the light of the origin.

The sovereignty of Prester John is the one of the Perfect Kingdom. It evolves, to a maximum degree, the motherly kindness and resting love appropriate to the kingdom of Cockaigne. But by raising them and brightening them with solar comprehension, an integration of the motherly side and the fatherly side, of the lunar aspect and the solar aspect, is carried out. Above all, it conciliates the instinctuality of Na-ture with the clear rationality of a superior principle of order.

A figure similar to Prester John is Sarastrus, the priest king of Mozart's (1756-1791) *Zauberfloete* (*The Magic Flute*). Its chant circumscribes, magically, the eternal kingdom of perfection: "Within these holy walls, / where men love their fellow men, / no traitor can lurk, / because we forgive our enemies."[101] Both figures own lunar peculiarities, joined to solar Nature. Both superintend, in humbleness, a kingdom which is synonymous with the complete circularity of unconsciousness.

Certainly, they are not alone and to them and to their "imaginal" lands, one could associate, the rulers and the reigns of many utopias: from Tommaso Campanella's (1568-1639) *The City of the Sun* to Thomas More's (1478-1535) *Utopia*, from Francis Bacon's (1561-1626) *New Atlantis,* to Francois Fenelon's (1651-1715) *Telemacus's Adventures*, to Moreilly's *Naufrage des Isles flottantes ou Basiliade*, to E. Cabet's *Journey to Icaria*,[102] to the modern and contemporary utopias. They all express, in different ways, what Prester John and Sarastrus openly reveal: the conscious yearning of man and mankind to return to the blissful *status* (condition) of the origins. And this is nothing else but the desire to blend with the *Unus Mundus*.

In other words, Prester John and Sarastrus, in their dominions, far from ideological waste and moralistic or edifying aims, visualize, in an archetypal form, the project of a balanced humankind and conciliated to its own experience of the deep; a unanimity which has conquered the full syntony between individual and cosmos.

But now one enters the field which Jung calls, with the ancient name syzygy, "the sphere of experience which takes directly to the experience of individuation, of becoming the Self."[103] It is where the integration between the unconscious and conscious takes place, both collectively and individually. It is the icon of the Perfect Kingdom of all eras.

3. Shadow in the Unconscious and in the Perfect Kingdom.

Distinctive signs in the land of Cockaigne, and later in the kingdom of Prester John, outline in the whole of their oneiric magnificence, the sphere of the *Unus Mundus*, of the unconscious integrated with the conscious. Symbolized by the *Grail*,[104] it reveals the great numinous light of the Self: the ordering center of the unconscious.[105] But the Perfect Kingdom, the kingdom of origins, the Grail kingdom, cannot be such if it does not include and integrate its dark side, its demoniacal and inexpressive side: its shadow. As the alchemical science teaches, there is no *coagula* if there is no *solve*.

Now the shadow is, certainly, an unconscious part of the individual personality. That is why it is somehow uncomfortable and annoying, and each time one encounters it, the tendency is to withdraw from it. "Each one of us," says Jung, "is followed by a shadow, and the least it is incorporated into the individual conscious life, the more it is dark and thick."[106] Due to its complexity, one may say of it both a *lectio facilitor* (easier lesson) and a *difficilior* (more difficult lesson). In the first case, the shadow may resolve into "something clumsy and primitive";[107] in the second case it may represent something fascinating and disturbing—the *umbra solis* (shadow of the sun).[108] In both cases, it cannot be removed. Otherwise, as poet Robert Bly says, it is as heavy as a sack, on the shoulders of the unfortunate who cannot or does not want to get rid of it.[109] It becomes a destiny full of affliction and regression which does not leave its prey, conditioning its thoughts and behavior.

Due to its personalization, the shadow can be associated with the witch, the stepmother, the devil, the ogre, or the wizard of folk tales.[110] Or it can materialize, as a terrifying nightmare, in dreams and in fantasies. It is, in other words, a presence which may become so impending as to possess the individual, turning him to its own wills. In most tales, the characters which end up dominated by an evil entity, are truly prisoners of the shadow.

If this is the obstacle that the individual will inevitably run into in his journey towards perfection (or the process of individuation), the same happens to the unconscious in its psychic unity, a *complexio oppositorum*. Because the collective unconscious is a vital, dynamic unity in eternal equilibrium,[111] if it wants to be a totality—it needs to be continually integrated by its dark side. On the other hand if it weren't a fundamental component of the unconscious, the shadow would not even exist as a personal archetype. "The personal Shadow," says Jung, "is, so as to say, the descendent of a collective numinous figure."[112] "The impurity of the world" is an important presence; "the light has a sense only where it enlightens darkness."[113] Without it, there could never be a totality.

That the archetype of the shadow exists, at a collective level and independent of its function in individuals, was also known to the alchemists. According to Jung, they discovered its "specific psychological existence," by making it a concrete reality, gifted of an eternal and incorruptible substance.[114] That this "eternal and incorruptible substance", which is the shadow, may not be integrated by the collective unconscious without disastrous consequences. It is what Jung perceived as that which happened to *Yahweh*, the God of the *Old Testament*: "He can project, with maximum indifference his 'shadow', and be unconscious of it, at the expense of human beings."[115]

This is not, however, easy to comprehend. Our consciousness and our culture are in rebellion against the hypothesis that perfection may have a dark side. It is unthinkable, a logical contradiction, a revelation that has always been stubbornly refused and confined to the "not said" or "unspeakable." It hides an existential insecurity, the terror of abandonment to obscure and uncontrollable forces, the fear of being devoured. It is the quintessence of each person's anguish of death, the sum of all the ancestral fears of humankind.[116]

Even if the difficulties in accepting it are enormous, it exists. Indeed, the fullness of the Self as a totality of the unconscious—the point of encounter between the individual, social group, Nature and culture—proclaims it. One can see this in the imaginal construction of the Perfect Kingdom—the kingdom of unconsciousness. In it, though hidden by symbolic redundancy, is the power the shadow exposes.

An example can be seen in Luciano's journey, in the form of an exceptional vineyard. The superior part of the trunk is formed by polyglot women, whose fingers and hair are arborescent. Their extraordinary sexuality addresses the unfortunate visitors, seducing them. Incapable of opposing the double fascination of the protective-motherly (the link between the tree and the earth) and the feminine-sexual, the visitors abandon themselves to the vine-women. Being clutched by the genitals, they are later transformed into vine-shoots and tendrils.[117] The extraordinary fertility of Nature, the symbol of the motherly and beneficial protection of the collective unconscious becomes, here, a mortal trap. The shadow inserts seductively where total freedom seems to be one with spontaneity and the satisfaction of every desire. But freedom

and desire can turn into devouring monsters, into a return to unconsciousness—the motherly-feminine—which coincides with the
annihilating whirlpool of the hermaphroditic *uroborus*. The horrible
mixture of living and arborescence goes back to the primitive *participation mystique*, where embryonal consciousness can be interchanged with
everything else, and where the senses are gifted with their own life.[118]

In the pacifying vision of the Perfect Kingdom, everyone's coveted
goal, there hides a dark side. For whoever seeks refuge there, be it an
individual or a community, nothing can be taken for granted. Even
what is most sacred or desirable may hide some danger.

If, with accurate attention, one observes the *Earthly Paradise* in
Hieronymus Bosch's (1453-1516) *Triptych: The Garden of Delights*, the
great fresco of the Perfect Kingdom, one may note a dystonic note. In
the paradisiacal harmony, the shadow of imperfection stands out, albeit
well camouflaged. Anthropomorphic cliffs, fantastic trees and animals
that devour each other, surround the fountain of life, on whose summit
the pagan-evil symbol of the half moon stands.[119] What by definition is
order; it is not to be separated from disorder and the absurd. As in the
Bardol Todol, the risk of falling in the *samsara* of the unconscious is
always there.[120]

Even in the kingdom of Prester John hides an unsuspected danger.
Men who feed on human flesh and consider it a "most sacred action"
testify with their presence that no value exists that may not be, negatively, transcended.[121] They are the people of *Gog* and *Magog*, ever since
considered troops of the Antichrist, seal of the Apocalypse, a materialization of impending doom, a true archetype of inhumanity.[122] They
are the living peril of a regression to a pre-conscious *status* (condition),
to a uroboric reality which denies distinction even if they are to devour
each other; cannibalism is always each other's meal. As a shadow of
man and mankind, it is a regressive possibility that aligns itself even in
a paradisiacal perfection. Contiguity with the completeness of the Self
does not avoid devouring choices and wicked temptations. It is the
transgressive way of an omnipotent delirium, itself a vehicle of the impulse of destruction and death.[123] Individuals and entire peoples have
been contaminated by it, historically, without being able to remove
themselves. Even in recent times possession by the Shadow has diverted,

tragically, nations and races from the route to perfection, in fooling those peoples into believing that they already have it. The Shadow loves to be a *trickster*.[124]

The Lord of the Perfect Kingdom bears its Shadow. In the same way it exists archetypally in the geographical antiphony of the sovereign of the paradisiacal kingdom. For Prester John the king-priest of a delight-ful garden—of a perfect and spiritual kingdom—can be associated with the sovereign-priest of a kingdom that is only apparently perfect, ap-parently Paradisiacal. He is the famous Old Man(or Venerable Man) of the Mountain,[125] the religious and political chief of the Ishmaelite sect, that arose in the eleventh century and was later destroyed by the invad-ing Mongolian sovereigns, but which remains alive, in many aspects, in the collective imagination. We know little about this sect called the *Assini* (from the Arabic *hasisiyyin*, or men devoted to the *hasis*). But Burchardus, a messenger of Frederick Barbarossa sent in 1175 to Egypt and Syria, gives news of it; and years later, William of Tyre (c.1130-c.1187) and Arnold of Lubeck's (d. between 1211 and 1214) *Chronicles* refer to it.[126] The story does not differ, except in small details, from the following testimony of Marco Polo (1254?-1324?).[127] It is told that there exists a wonderful garden in which flowers, fruit trees, animals, foun-tains of milk, honey and wine surround golden palaces, where the seduction of the flesh mixes with the seductions of Nature. In this *fac simile* of the Koranic Paradise, youngsters, educated and bold, are in-troduced into it under the influence of *hashish*. They believe they are experiencing the Koranic Paradise. At their awakening the Old Man of the Mountain asks them to be blind instruments of his will, if they want to go back to it.[128] Remarkable in this chronicle, where the leg-endary becomes real and the real becomes a legend, is the turning negative of everything in the land of Prester John that is noble and harmonic.

Nature hides in its beauty the most pernicious danger. While it con-tains higher qualities that are at the service of what goes beyond evil itself, evil consumes Nature, seemingly without sense. In the *Novellino*, at a simple gesture of the Old Man, two youngsters from his sect show blind obedience to him by jumping from a tower, killing themselves.[129] The wisdom of old age, the harmony of sovereignty, turns into a negative shadow; it becomes senseless, abusive, evil and violent. It is the negation of every order. From the astonishing report of Burchardus, one learns that the followers of the *Assassini* (murderers) sect lie with their mothers and sisters, infringing on, by committing incest, the principle of each social order.[130]

The primordial, dark image is designed; it is the image of the Collective Unconscious, lacking all sort of distinctive form, all sort of *logos*.[131] It is a land not yet enlightened by the sun of conscience. The Old Man, whom in this kingdom is the absolute Lord, is the wizard of the tales, the demon of the myths, the heavy sack on ones shoulders, not noticing it and refusing to notice it. As if under a spell, everything that is in the power is *arcanum* (occult) and ambiguous, objectifies and shows itself: becomes the "evil facade of power."[132]

The dark side of the kingdom is not eliminable. Its presence being connected to the structure of the unconscious it does not dissolve, even when the Perfect Kingdom ideologizes in the form of utopia. One finds in recent times, the Shadow in the figure of the Big Brother in the prophetic novel *1984* by George Orwell (1903-1950),[133] wherein its technological manipulation is a substitute for the shrewdness of the "Old Man of the Mountain." And, with more clarity the mysterious "Great Old Man" appears as the unsuspectable guide of international terrorism: a sort of double darkness of power.

They are all modern personifications of the immortal "Old Man of the Mountain": they disturb the tranquillity of those whom live in a satisfying *a priori*. It is the *a priori* of those who refuse the heavy sack which weighs on the shoulders of mankind. Those who think (or wish) perfection to be a *continuum* (continuity), conquered by the virtues of culture and progress, are like those who would live in a paradisiacal kingdom which lacks shadows because it lacks light. With these optics the paradisiacal kingdom of perfection dissolves into the ocean of the unreachable. If reached, it reveals as the "hell in music" by Bosch, the representation of the shadow, of the abyss of nothingness: *"eripitur persona, manet res."*

4. True Harmony or the Perfect Regalness.

In Medieval times and in later centuries, a musical tune is the source of many worries for composers. It is the *diabolus in musica*, so called because of it's difficult intonation and its unbearable dissonance.[134] Like the shadow it shows itself with an evil aura, somewhat disturbing. The *diabolus in musica* stops disturbing composers after the nineteenth century, when the dissonance does not arouse fear. On the contrary, then there might be a possibility of reaching harmony.

This is the shadow's arcane way to possess it once again. Such possession is fundamental to the process of individuation.[135] A process which, alone, may take the individual and the collective to a totality and harmony of the Self; to become old and wise, masters of the meaning of life, thus the real Lords of the Perfect Kingdom.[136] But this requires a radical transformation. It is a transformation that involves the individual, others, and the political and social relationships which connect them all. The process of individuation, consciously carried out, modifies, in the words of Marie-Louise von Franz, "even the ordinary sphere of the individual's human relations."[137]

Reflecting oneself in the Shadow, of confronting shadow in oneself, is requisite for being conscious of its eliminative existence, for integrating it with consciousness. This dynamic, acceptable, even though harsh, to the individual, shows itself as impossible to the collective. Blocking it is the neurotic fear that there might be no certainty, no secure cavern in which to hide. One of the strongest and most famous chants of the Lutheran Reform, by J. S. Bach, opens with an impassioned and nostalgic confession, *"Ein fest Burg ist unser Gott* (a mighty stronghold is our God still). "* It is the projection of a desire to have a secure shelter where the Self lives—uncontaminated by the Shadow.

To think that the negative is an integral part of living Nature, in the center of creation, means that the shadow penetrates to the deepest nucleus of the numinous, into its *mysterium tremendum* (tremendous secret).[138] It means raising to consciousness the experience of the mystic, of the illuminated, of the initiated, to the Mosaic vision of the darkness of the light.[139] The experience in which, according to Gregory of Nyssa, the real and full knowledge reveals itself; in which it is always a "seeing in blindness, because we are looking for what goes beyond our knowledge, surrounded on each side by misunderstanding and darkness."[140] It is like penetrating into the region of the *complexio oppositorum*, a home where there is no rationality, where the logic of non-contradiction fails, and where dissonance can destroy the unlucky one who does not understand its hidden harmony.

To integrate the Shadow is like the effort of the hero who overcomes the dragon in the mild and secret conflicts of the human soul, or of Parsifal who goes beyond reluctance and asks the venerated king the decisive question. Like the effort which sets Parsifal free from his regressive narcissism, or sets the *Grail* king free from the shadow-wound, the origin of shame, desolation and pain.[141]

The discovery of the Shadow in the Perfect Kingdom is akin to the realization, in the Cain/Abel myth, of the archetypal power of death, the great shadow of humanity.[142] Similarly the Shadow livens up the life of unconsciousness, taking it to be the Self, "the psychic totality of man."[143] It is possible for human beings to rise to a fullness that is different from the undifferentiatedness of the primordial phase of unconsciousness. But full consciousness is aware of both the determining and non-determining influences from the unconscious. "The psychological idea of the Self…is born from a union of the conscious with the unconscious."[144]

Evil in perfection is the seal of a fundamental and uncomfortable truth. The truth seen in the Old Man of the Mountain, by the other aspect of Prester John, in the way which society and culture reflect themselves in their instinctive aspects, where the original and wild lurks in man and man-kings as its hidden nature. To recognize its presence, to integrate the Shadow, is to discover the unspeakable, that everything runs to become a unity: *"omnia in unum convertit"* (everything changes itself in one and the same thing). That the alchemical *nigredo* changes into *albedo*, the transmutative miracle of the mythical *Phoenix*,[145] who in order to triumph, changes into *rubedo*: the Living Opera, the Incorruptible Body, the *Filius Philosophorum*, the *Sol Invictus*, the light of consciousness "which starts to react even at the emotive level as to the contents produced by the unconscious."[146]

This is why perfection of the kingdom, like power, has an instinctual aspect, violent and bloody. It is its shadow and its absolute and eliminative need. Without it, the *albedo* and the *rubedo* of psychological projection do not verify. Wherefore it is not possible to reach the Self. "Without the integration of evil," says Jung, "there is no totality."[147] So what appears scandalous is congruent, that the shadow walks with wisdom, rationality and luminosity. Their *coniunctio* is the seal of perfection and totality. It is the sovereignty that forever renews in the tension between conscious and unconscious, in order to integrate with the Self; it is the *Rex* (king), old and young in one.[148] It is the perfect and fulfilled *complexio*, the *Rex* shows his being *supra partere* (upper part), his being *Rex Supremus* (supreme king) or *Imperator* (emperor).

In all symbolic traditions, the *Rex Supremus* or *Imperator* represent the center of the world, the guarantor of universal renewal (*cakravartin*).[149] As the center of an ideal *mandala* which encloses the sky and the earth, it symbolizes the fullness of perfection; the one which unconsciousness has to reach, every time, in every man and mankind, by joining in marriage is consciousness.

Its archetypal figure is the androgynous "father of everything" of the gnosis,[150] it is the *Rex* of the *Unus Mundus*: the world of origins, which, enlightened by the light of consciousness, must become our world, the desired earthly Jerusalem, the Perfect Kingdom. Everyone, of course, must become the *Rex Supremus* to himself and the world, and to find out that the boundaries of the paradisiacal kingdom are traced by him and to him only if it is given the possibility of penetrating into what is his mystical body, his "imaginary land."

He will find himself to be in the archetypal dimension, whose representation is given by Bosch's *Triptych: The Garden of Delights*.[151] Here, the timeless imaginative oneirical richness, the shadow of the unconscious perfectly integrated with the light of consciousness, unfolds in the harmony of the *complexio*, of each *complexio*. The naked figures, masculine and feminine, black and white, which define on the left and on the right side of the inferior part of the board, which are all figures of the *complexio*, correspond, in the superior part near the top of the mystical triangle, to the fountain of youth. But it does not show the boundary of the Perfect Kingdom. It is rather the beginning of something unknown, unrepresentable, which stands at the horizon and which is a natural continuation and completion of the Perfect Kingdom, the paradisiacal kingdom.

At the end of the gnostic *Apocalypse,* Peter says, "At present there is no place in men who are not immortal, but only in those whom have been chosen because of their immortal nature, and in whom have shown to be capable of receiving it."[152]

Notes

1   Augustine, *De civitate Dei*, Rome, 1978, Bk IV, chp 4, vol I, pp. 256-57.

2   From the Latin verb *removeo*. This verb possesses a high personifying attitude— to remove, to send away, to dismiss. By using it in the context of justice, Augustine wants to highlight its personal and independent dimension, which reveals its archetypal nature.

3   "In the first place we talked about a just government, and this was to differentiate between the States and the bands of preditors and pirates, with whom we shall keep no relationship, no commerce, no alliance. " J. Bodin, *I sei libri dello Stato*, Italian translation, Turin, 1964, vol I, Bk I, chp 1, p. 160.

4   See M. Garcia-Pelayo, *El reino de Dios, arquetipo politico: Estudio sobre las formas politicas de la alta edad media*, Madrid, 1959, p. 40ff.

5   Milton, *Paradiso perduto*, Italian translation, Milan, 1990, lines 641-42, p. 582.

6   On the nostalgia for Paradise, see G. H. Williams, *Wilderness and Paradise in Christian Thought*, New York, 1962.

7   See Mircea Eliade, *Mito e realta*, Italian translation, Rome, 1966, p. 76ff; G. van der Leeuw, *Fenomenologia della religione*, Italian translation, Turin, 1992, pp. 451ff.

8   See S. Donaldoni, *Storia della letteratura egiziana antica*, Milan, 1959, p. 78.

9   Homer, *Odissea*, Italian translation, 2nd edition, Milan, 1976, lines 563-69, pp. 92-93.

10   Hesiod, "Opere e giorni," in *Opere*, Turin, 1977, lines 90-125, pp. 254-57.

11   Publius Virgilius Maro, "Quarta Bucolica," in *Opere*, Turin, 1971, lines 5-47, pp. 98-103.

12   Luke 23. 43 (King James Version).

13   "Qur'an," Sutra 2. 23, translated by E. H. Palmer, in *The Sacred Books of the East*, Oxford, 1880, vol VI.

14   See Ezekiel 28. 13-14/47. 12; Isaiah 11. 6-10/41. 17-20, 60-61; Hosea 14; Joel 2. 18-27; Amos 9. 11-15; Zephaniah 3. 9-20; Publio Ovidio Nasone, *Metamorfosi*, Milan, 1992, Bk I, lines 89-112, pp. 10-13.

15   On Paradise as an "inside out" world, see G. Cochiara, *Il mondo alla rovescia*, Turin, 1963.

16   See A. Graf, "Il mito del paradiso terrestre," in *Miti, leggende e superstizioni del medioevo*, Milan, 1984, p. 47.

17   Revelation 21.9-27.

18   The word *edinu* or *edin*, borrowed from the Accadian or Sumerian language, means desert. In Hebrew, *eden* means the opposite; it is a luxuriant garden, full of animals. This is why in Greek it has been translated with the term *paradeisos*, park, garden. See A. M. Gerard, *Dizionario della Biblia*, Italian translation, Milan, 1994, vol I, p. 379ff; H. B. Partin, "Paradise," in *The Encyclopedia of Religion*, edited by Mircea Eliade, New York, 1987, vol XI, pp. 184-89.

19   On the meaning of the symbols used, see Mircea Eliade, *Trattato di storia della religion*, Italian translation, 4th edition, Padua, 1988; J. C. Cooper, *Dizionario dei simboli*, Italian translation, 2nd edition, Padua, 1988; M. M. Davy, *Il simbolismo medievale*, Italian translation, Rome, 1988; J. Chevalier and A. Gheerbrant, *Dizionario delle mitologie e delle religioni*, Italian translation, 5th edition, Milan, 1989, vols I, II; Y. Bonnefoy, *Dizionario delle mitologie e della religione*, Italian translation, Milan, 1989, vols I, II, III; R. Guenon, *Simboli della scienza sacra*, Italian translation, Milan 1990; H. Biedermann, *Enciclopedia dei simboli*, Italian translation, 1991; Joseph Campbell, *Le figure del mito*, Italian translation, Como, 1991; G. van der Leeuw, *op cit*; A. M. Gerard, *op cit*, vols I, II.

20   See Carl Gustav Jung, "Mysterium coniunctionis, Ricerche sulla separazione e composizione negli opposti psichici nell'alchimia," Italian translation, in *Opere*, Turin, 1991, vol XIV, pp. 463-66. On the *Unus Mundus*, see Marie Louise von Franz, *L'unus mundus e l'incontro delle diverse realta in Le tracce del futuro divinazione e tempo*, Italian translation, Como, 1986, pp. 132-54.

21   See Jung, "Mysterium coniunctionis," *Opere*, vol XIV, pp. 532-42.

22   Dante Alighieri, *Divina Commedia*, Florence, 1963, vol III, Paradiso, canto XXXIII. 124-26, pp. 415-16.

23   See Tauler, "Il canto della nudita," in Martin Buber, *Confessioni estatiche*, Italian translation, Milan, 1987, pp. 129-30.

24   Johann Wolfgang von Goethe, *Faust*, Milan, 1965, vol I, pp. 24-25.

25   For the term "imaginal," see Henry Corbin, *Spiritual Body and Celestial Earth: A Study of Persian Mysticism*, translated from the French by Nancy Pearson, Princeton, 1977.

26   See J. H. S. Armstrong, *The Paradise Myth*, London, 1969.

27   In T. H. Gaster, *Le piu antiche storie del mondo*, Italian translation, Milan, 1971, p. 47.

28   See Corbin, *ibid*, p. 270, n 41; and E. B. Moyniahn, *Paradise as a Garden: in Persia and Mughal India*, New York, 1979.

29   See E. Frola, *Il piu grande dialogo del Nirvana definitivo* (Mahaparinibbanasuttanta), Milan, 1995, pp. 103-04.

30   See V. Psani, *Mahabharata, Episodi scelti*, Turin, 1968, pp. 63-64.

31   See B. Branston, *Gli Dei del Nord*, Italian translation, Milan, 1991, *passim e partic.*, p. 197.

32   The Perfect Kingdom is somewhat spacial: its research will be a constant, especially in the Western world. See J. Delumeau, *Storia del paradiso: Il giardino delle delizie*, Italian translation, Bologna, 1994. It presents itself at the same time as the moment of origin, the first act of creation, and its point of arrival.

33   On the position of earthly Paradise, see Graf, *op cit*, pp. 45-56.

34   Plato, *Politico*, Italian translation, 3rd edtion, Milan, 1992, sections 271E-272B, pp. 331-32.

35   See Pindar, "Il Olympique," in *Olympiques*, Paris, 1970, lines 112-36, p. 46.

36   Joseph Campbell, *Mitologia creativa: Le maschere di Dio*, Italian translation, Milan, 1992, vol II, p. 752ff.

37   See Hesiod, "Teogonia," in *Opere*, lines 214-17, pp. 72-73.

38   Quinto Orazio Flacco, "Gli Epodi," in *Le opere*, 2nd edition, Turin, 1969, lines 41-65, pp. 79-81

39   See Joseph Campbell, *Tra oriente e occidente*, Italian translation, Como, 1993, p. 14.

40   See A. Graf, *op cit*, p. 58.

41   *Ibid*, p. 66ff.

42   See Delumeau, *op cit*, p. 177ff.

43   The boldness which supports research makes of a man an heroic figure. But the hero is nothing but just: *the* just man.

44   On the Christian conception of Paradise, see H. Leclercq, "Paradis," in *Dictionnaire d'archeologie chretienne et de liturgie*, F. Cabrol, editor, Paris, 1938, tome XIII, deuxieme partie, c 1578-1615; J. Hekel, P. Hoffmann, K. Rahner, "Paradies," in J. Hoefer, K. Rahner, editors, *Lexikon fuer Theologie und Kirche*, Freiberg in B. , 1963, band VIII, c 67-72; P. Miquel, "Paradis," in *Dictionnaire de spiritualite ascetique et mistique doctrine et histoire*, Paris, 1984, tome XII, primiere partie, cc 187-197.

45   See Justin, "Cohortatio ad Graecos," in J. P. Migne, *Patrologiae Cursus completus -Series Graeca*, Paris, 1884, tome VI, c 294; Tertullian, "Apologeticus adversus gentes pro christianis," chp XLVII, 520, in J. P. Migne, *Patrologiae Cursus Completus-Series Latina*, Paris, 1878, tome I, c 587; and Lactantius, "Divinarum institutionum," libri septem, liber II, chp XIII, in J. P. Migne, *ibid, Series Latina*, Paris, 1844, tomus VI, c 32.

46   See Basil di Cesarea, *Sulla Genesi (Omelie sull'Esamerone)*, Milano, 1990; and Pseudo-Basil, *"De hominis structura,"* Oratio III, De Paradiso, (Appendix Tomi I Operum Sancti Basilii Magni), 347D-351D, in J. P. Migne, *op cit, Series Graeca*, Paris, 1888, tomus XXX, cc 62-72.

47   To reach the paradisiacal kingdom/Lucky Islands and drink of the fount from which the greatest rivers of the world are born, means to reach eternal life immediately—not *post mortem*.

48   See Delumeau, *op cit*, p. 25ff.

49   See Ididore di Seville, "Etymologiarum libri XX," liber XIV, caput VI, Bff, in J. P. Migne, *op cit, Series Latina*, Paris, 1887, tomus LXXXII, c 514ff. Later, Isidore will adopt one of Augustine's "realistic" positions, thus toning down his doubts, *"De ordine creaturarum liber,"* caput X (7-11), in J. P. Migne, *ibid*, Paris, 1862, tomus LXXXIII, cc 939-940.

50   Augustine, *La Genesi II-La Lenesi alla lettera*, Rome, 1989, liber VIII, 7, 13, pp. 406-07.

51   Mauro, "De Universo libri viginti duo," liber XII, caput V, D, in J. P. Migne, *op cit, Series Latina*, Paris, 1864, tomus CXI, c 354. Although Mauro here says that the Lucky Islands have been confused with Paradise, in liber II, caput III, cc 334-454, he describes Paradise as if it was the Lucky Islands. See Lombard, *"Sententiarum libri quatuor,"* liber II, dist XVII, 5-6, in J. P. Migne, *ibid*, Paris, 1880, tomus CXCII, cc 686-87.

52   Aquinas, "Summa Theologiae," pars prima, qu 102, ar I, arg 4, in *Opera omnia*, R. Busa, editor, Stuttgart, 1980, vol II, p. 330.

53   See *La navigazione di San Brandano*, Italian translation, Palermo, 1992, p. 109ff. For its later popularization in the 12th century, see Benedeit, *Il viaggio di San Brandano*, Parma, 1994, pp. 150-157.

54   On this secular journey, see Delumeau, *op cit*, chps 5-8, pp. 129-232.

55   See Voltaire, *Dizionario filosofico*, Italian translation, Milan, 1968, pp. 336-37.

56   See "Paradise," in *Enciclopedia o dizionario ragionato della scienza, delle arti e dei mesteri (1751-1772)*, Italian translation, Milan, 1966, vol II, p. 458.

57   On the figure of the *honnete homme*, see F. Jesi, "Honnete homme," "homme de bien," *"grand homme,"* in *Cultura di destra: Il linguaggio delle "idee senza parole,"* Milan, 1979, p. 130.

58   See Rousseau, *Discorso sull'origine e I fondamenti della in eguaglianza tra gli uomini*, Italian translation, Rome, 1971, p. 102ff.

59   Kant, "Congetture sull'origine della storia," in *Scritti politici e della filosofia della storia e del diritto*, Italian translation, Turin, 1956, pp. 201-02. The entire essay is significant.

60   It is enough to remember the ideological political propaganda, which at the time of the Cold War, made the USA the Paradise of freedom, and the socialism of the USSR the place of newborn civilization.

61   See Dante, "Inferno," in *Divina Comedia*, 12th edition, Florence, 1962, canto XXVI. 85-142, pp. 297-302.

62   See Jung, "Fenomelogia dello apirito nella fiable," in *Opere*, Italian translation, 3rd edition, Turin, 1988, vol 9, tome I; "Introduzione all'inconscio," in *L'uomao e I suoi simboli*, Italian translation, Milan, 1980, pp. 5-87. Erich Neumann, *Storia delle origini della origini della conscienza*, Italian translation, Rome, 1978. von Franz, *L'individuation nella fiaba*, Italian translation, Turin, 1987; *Le fiabe del lieto fine:*

Psicologia della storie di redenzione, Italian translation, Como, 1987; *Le fiabe interpretate,* Italian translation, 6th edition, Turin, 1992. H. von Beit, *Symbolik des Maerchens* and *Gegensatz und Enneurung im Maerchen,* Bern, 1952 and 1956.

63 Mysterious and uncertain is the etymology of the name. Depending on the instances, it refers to a castle, to a real or poetic character. The oldest work in which it is mentioned belongs to the 13th century: *Li fabliaus de Coquaigne.* See Graf, *op cit,* p. 145; G. Cocchiara, *Il paese di Cuccagna,* Turin, 1956, notes on chp 5, pp. 248-49.

64 See Lucian, *Storia vera,* Italian translation, 2nd edition, Milan, 1993. Typical characteristics of the kingdom of Cockaigne or Bengodi are also found in Metagene's comedy *Turiopersi* and in Ferecrate's *Minatori.* See Cocchiara, *op cit,* p. 181.

65 Lucian, *op cit,* bk II, lines 11-14, pp. 116-19.

66 Lucian says about the sexual habits of the people of the Islands of the Blissful, ". . . they join up openly before everybody, with females and males, and they don't think it shameful. " *Ibid,* bk II, line 19, pp. 124-105.

67 See *Il Corano,* sura XLIV, 51-55, pp. 368-69; sura LII, 20, p. 394; sura LV, 56-58, p. 405; sura LVI, 22-25, p. 406; sura LXXVIII, 33, p. 457.

68 See "Li fablianus de Coquaigne," in *Fabliaux: racconti comici medioevali,* G. C. Belletti, editor, Ivrea, 1982, pp. 94-105.

69 Boccaccio, *Decamerone,* Turin, 1975, VIII, 3, p. 703ff.

70 For a complete review of the texts and popular poems on the kingdom of Cockaigne or of Bengodi, see Cocchiara, *op cit,* pp. 160-171.

71 This is the direction taken, at least partially, by P. Camporesi, *Il paese della fame,* 2nd editon, Bologna, 1985, pp. 71-116.

72 On the Collective Unconscious as Uroborus, see Erich Neumann, *Storia delle origini della coscienza,* pp. 27-103; and *La Grande Madre: Fenomenologia delle configurazioni femminili dell'inconsio,* Italian translation, Rome, 1981.

73 See Jung, "Gli aspetti psicologici dell'archetipo della madre," in *Opere,* vol 9, tome I, p. 83ff.

74 "No kingdom" means the refusal of power as a hierarchical ascent strongly rationalized and ordered. The power exercised from the motherly archetype, though being absolute and unconditional, shows itself as emotive and pulsional.

75 See Pieter Brueghel, *L'opera completa,* Milan, 1967, tables XLIV-XLV, and p. 109.

76 See T. Manteuffel, *Nascita dell'eresia,* Italian translation, Florence, 1975; Norman Cohn, *I fanatici dell'Apocalisse,* Italian translation, Milan, 1965; G. G. Merlo, *Eretici ed eresie medioevali,* Bologna, 1989.

77 See G. D. H. Cole, *Storia del pensiero socialista,* Italian translation, Bari, vols I-V, 1967-1973; also, L. Pellicani, *I rivoluzionari di professione,* Florence, 1975.

78 See *La terra madre e dea: Sacralita della natura che ci fa vivere-Quaderni di Eranos,* Italian translation, Como, 1989; and particularly Erich Neumann, *Il significato dell'architipo della terra nell'era moderna,* pp. 21-65.

79   On the complex events tied to this letter, its reception, its importance, and its slight credibility, see G. Zaganelli, *Introduzione e Nota informativa a La lettera di Prete Gianni*, Parma, 1990, pp. 7-49; Pirenne, *La legende du Pretre Jean*, Strasbourg, 1992; and Delumeau, *op cit*, pp. 97-128.

80   See *La lettera di Prete Gianni*, pp. 54-55.

81   *Ibid.*

82   *Ibid*, p. 58ff, 82ff, 90ff.

83   See L. Bianco, *Le pietre mirabili: Magia e scienza nei lapidari greci*, Palermo, 1992.

84   See *La letter di Prete Gianni*, p. 56ff.

85   *Ibid*. This theme appears both in the classical form of the fountain, pp. 60ff, 88ff, and in the form of a spring from a tree, p. 62ff. In the latter case the symbolism of water as a source of eternal youth, together with the tree which is the union of the sky and earth, highlights the character of the symbolized regenerative totality. See Jung, "Mysterium coniunctionis," p. 70ff. *Cf* the Nordic tradition: the ash tree's fountain *Yggdrasil* of the *Volospa* in the *Edda*.

86   See *La lettera di Prete Gianni*, p. 62ff.

87   Jung, "Mysterium coniunctionis," p. 290.

88   *Ibid.*

89   *La lettera di Prete Gianni*, pp. 66-67.

90   See Neumann, *Storia delle origini della coscienza*, p. 359.

91   Jung, "Mysterium coniunctionis," p. 390.

92   Jung, "Psicologia e religione," in *Opere*, Italian translation, vol XI, Turin, 1992, p. 222.

93   What is hermaphroditic-uroboric refers to the hyperprotective motherly character of the unconscious from which the process of individuation must begin, to end in the Self, as a totality of the unconscious in perfect equilibrium. See Neumann, *Storia delle origini della coscienza*, p. 359.

94   *La lettera di Prete Gianni*, pp. 76-77.

95   *Ibid*, p. 85.

96   Iranaeus of Lyon, *Contro le eresie*, Italian translation, Siena, 1968, vol I, XX, pp. 26-27.

97   Jung, "Mysterium coniunctionis," p. 17.

98   Jung, "Il simbolo della trasformazione nella messa," in *Opere*, vol XI, p. 268.

99   See the old French version in *La lettera di Prete Gianni*, pp. 168-99, and particularly pp. 198-99.

100 *Ibid*, pp. 92-93.

101 "In queste sacre mura / dove l'uomo, / il traditore non insidia, / poiche al nemico si perdona," Mozart-Schikaneder, *Il flauto magico*, Milan, 1975, pp. 146-47.

102 See Campanella, *La citta del sole*, Milan, 1962; More, *L'utopia o la ligliore forma di repubblica*, Italian translation, Bari, 1966; Bacon, *"Nuova Atlantide,"* in *Scritti politici giuridici e storici*, Italian translation, Turin, 1971, vol I, pp. 779-827; F. Fenelon de Salignac de La Mothe, *Le aventure di Telemaco*, Italian translation, Turin, 1959; Moreilly, *Naufrag des Isles flottantes ou Basiliade du celebre Pilpai*, Messina, 1753, 2 vols; Cabet, *Viaggio in Icaria*, Italian translation, Naples, 1983; J. Harrington, *La repubblicca di Oceania*, Italian translation, Milan, 1985.

103 Jung, "Aspetti psicologici dell'archetipo della madre," p. 205.

104 On the symbolic identity between the Grail and Paradise, see Guenon, *Simboli della Sciencza sacra*, p. 25ff.

105 Jung, "Psicologia della figura del Briccone," in *Opere*, vol XI, tomo I, p. 293.

106 Jung, "Psicologia e religione," p. 82.

107 *Ibid*, p. 84.

108 Jung, "Mysterium coniunctionis," p. 125.

109 See Bly, *Il piccolo libro dell'ombra guida alla scoperta del nostro lato oscuro*, Italian translation, Como, 1992, p. 33ff.

110 See von Franz, *"Il processo di individuazione,"* in Jung, *L'uomo e I suoi simboli*, p. 154ff.

111 Jung, "Mysterium coniunctionis," p. 102.

112 Jung, "Psicologia della figura del Briconne," p. 254.

113 Jung, "Il simbolo della trasformazione nella messa," p. 274.

114 Jung, "Mysterium coniunctionis," p. 122.

115 Jung, "Risposta a Giobbe," in *Opere*, vol XI, p. 360.

116 See von Franz, "Il processo di individuazione," p. 194.

117 Lucian, *op cit*, pp. 60-63.

118 Lucien Levy-Bruhl, *L'anima primitiva*, Italian translation, Turin, 1992.

119 See H. Bosch, *L'opera completa*, 3rd edition, Milan, 1968, tables XXIV-XXVI, and p. 100.

120 See *Il libro tibetano dei morti*, Italian translation, Milan, 1988.

121 *La lettera di Prete Gianni*, pp. 54-57.

122 On the relationship between Prester John and the people of Gog and Magog, see A. Graf, *Roma nella memoria e nelle immaginazioni del Medio Evo*, Turin, 1883, vol II, pp. 507-63. On the apocalyptic character of God and Magog, see Ezekiel 38ff, and Revelation 20. 7-9. On the historical-symbolic importance of Gog and Magog, see E. Sackur, *Sibillynische Texte und Forschungen*, Halle, 1898, p. 92; A. R. Anderson, *Alexander's Gate, Gog and Magog and the Enclosed Nations*, Cambridge (Massachussetts), 1932; and Martin Buber, *Gog und Magog*, Frankfurt und Hamburg, 1957.

123 Of great interest is what Mircea Eliade writes in *La nascita mistica: Riti e simboli d'iniziazione*, 3rd edition, Italian translation, Brescia, 1988, pp. 103, 130.

124 See Jung, "Psicologia della figura del Brisccone," p. 254.

125 The strange epithet of the "Old Man of the Mountain" is not due to age, rather to an ambiguous translation from Arabic *Sayh*, sheik, which means both ruler and old. The choice "old" is due to the authority given to elders, or to the unconscious reference negatively given to the archetype of the "senex."

126 See Arnoldo di Lubecca, *Chronicon Slavorum*, 8th edition, VII; and W. Wattenbach, in *Deutschlands Geschichtesquellen*, Stuttgart-Berlin, 1970, vol II, p. 240. On the Old Man of the Mountain and the sect of the Assassins, see B. Lewis, *The Assassins, a Radical Sect in Islam*, London, 1967; and P. Filippani-Ronconi, *Ismaeliti ed "Assassini,"* Milan, 1973.

127 It recurs also in *Viagi del Beato Oderico da Pordenone*, Milan, 1931, p. 237; and in *I viaggi di Gionvanni da Mandavilla*, F. Zambrini, editor, Bologna, 1968, pp. 150-59.

128 See Marco Polo, *Il Milione*, Rome, 1982, chps 40-42, pp. 87-90.

129 See *Novellino e Conti del Duecento*, Turin, 1983, novel C, pp. 212-13.

130 See Arnoldo di Lubecca, *op cit.*

131 On the problem of the undistinct and passage to the distinct, see C. Bonvecchio, "Logos, Mythos, Nomos," in *L'immaginario e il potere*, G. M. Chiodi, editor, Turin, 1992, pp. 64-72.

132 This definition which recalls a famous book by G. Ritter, *Il volto demoniaco del potere*, Italian translation, Bologna, 1958, may be considered a debate on politics and morals. A debate which may be read as a political-philosophical transcription of the shadow problem.

133 Orwell, *1984*, Italian translation, Milan, 1973.

134 It is the tritone, the interval of the exiting fourth or of the diminishing fifth. See *La musica-Parte seconda-Dizionario*, Turin, 1968, vol I, p. 524.

135 See Jung, "Saggio d'interpretazione psicologia del dogma della Trinita," in *Opere*, vol XI, p. 191.

136 See Jung, "Mysterium coniunctionis," p. 222.

137 Von Franz, "Il processo di individuazione," p. 199.

138 See Rudolf Otto, *Il Sacro: L'irrazionale nella idea del divino e la sua relazione al razionale*, Italian translation, Milan, 1966, p. 22ff.

139 It is the experience of the darkness which allows us to pick up the light as shown in *Exodus* 19. 16-18.

140 Gregory of Nyssa, *La vita di Mose*, Milan, 1984, bk II, 163, pp. 154-55.

141 On the Parsifal event from the perspective of the process of individuation, see C. Rise, *Parsifal l'iniziazione machile alla donna e l'amore*, Como, 1988.

142 On the myth of Cain, see C. Bonvecchio, "Il segne di Caino come archetipo del potere," in *La contesa fra fratelli*, G. M. Chiodi, editor, Turin, 1992, pp. 67-109.

143 This definition is in Jung, "Saggio d'interpretazione psicologia del dogma della Trinita," p. 155.

144 Jung, "Mysterium coniunctionis," p. 378.

145 *Ibid*, pp. 77, 324.

146 *Ibid*, pp. 218-19.

147 Jung, "Saggio d'interpretazione psicologica del dogma della Trinita," p. 155.

148 Jung, "Mysterium coniunctionis," p. 292ff.

149 See M. Garcia Pelayo, *Miti e simboli politici*, Italian translation, Turin, 1970, pp. 9-69; and *El reino de Dios, arquetipo politico*, p. 101ff.

150 See Mircea Eliade, *Mefistofele e l'androgine*, Italian translation, Rome, 1989, pp. 71-114.

151 Bosch, *op cit*, tables XXIV-XXV, XXXVII.

152 "Apocalyse of Peter," in *Le Apocalissi gnostiche*, Milan, 1987, p. 30.

MICHIYOSHI HAYASHI

THE PATERNAL PRINCIPLE
AND ECONOMIC DEVELOPMENT

The capitalist society which began in Western Europe in the 17th century has continuously pursued happiness through technological advance and economic development. Aside from a difference in the way they distributed wealth, the socialist nations in the 20th century also pursued happiness by means of technological advance and economic development. Today, these socialist nations are making rapid shifts to a market economy. capitalism appears to have gained a victory over socialism; and the principles of capitalism are attempting to take control of the market on a global scale. It is a new form of capitalism characterized by mass production, mass consumption, with mass society as its background. Global capitalism promises material wealth and aims to create a comfortable and happy life-style. In advanced capitalist countries these goals have been met to some degree, with a hope in the possibility of a complete achievement very much alive.

Accompanying this worldwide shift toward mass capitalism is a worldwide increase in the corruption of morals. In the United States, for example, murders are commonplace in the illegal drug trade. Attempting to solve this problem by increasing police powers and legislating gun control has failed miserably, because it mistakes the means for the end. The root cause is moral corruption, of which the misuse of drugs and weapons are mere symptoms.

In ex-Communist countries, such as Russia and China, moral emptiness is also accompanying the shift to a market economy. Leading members of the Communist Party, who belonged to a privileged class up to now, are using their advantages to obtain powerful positions, in banking for example, to create a greater disparity between the classes than existed under the Communists. A number of those belonging to the new poorer classes are now becoming members of Mafia-like organizations that threaten the entire society with bribery and injustice.

At the heart of this moral corruption is a decline in the the Paternal Principle, which manifests itself in the need for order and rules. Without a the Paternal Principle at work, rules and order loose their importance. Sensitivity toward the care of others is lessened, as well as a decline in the ability for self-control.

Under the conditions of mass society the the Paternal Principle is something of a nuisance. Without it the morality of society collapses, and the world-scale disasters caused by immoral man will be frequent. In material terms, advanced capitalism appears to hold out a promise of perfect happiness. But behind this encouraging appearance is also a promise of the spiritual destruction of morality. To establish a sound and lasting order on this earth, where all are about to come together as one closely connected society, it is necessary for us to become involved in the phenomenon of the the Paternal Principle.

1. What is the the Paternal Principle?

The the Paternal Principle can be interpreted in a variety of ways, as leadership, power, authority, spirituality, the ability to see at a distance with a bird's-eye-view. I am envisioning it as a constituting ability; that is to say, the ability to join together various elements in order to create a meaningful whole, along with the ability to pass down that constituted culture to the next generation. This constituting ability obviously contains a moral aspect, for moral values are kept in mind when considering how the various elements should be joined together in a meaningful whole.

Whether a person possesses this the Paternal Principle or not can be determined by two methods: sand play and picture therapy. In sand play, people who have a constituting ability are able to create a scene viewed from their own perspective or to come up with a tale which is centered upon a character other than themselves. People who lack the

Paternal Principle, do not have the ability organize a meaningful whole. Such people can only see unrelated parts, which they fail to place in any kind of order with a unifying theme. Picture therapy, or the "scenery depicting," is a method developed in Japan to discern constituting ability through sketching. Participants are asked to sketch ten objects in the following order: river, mountain, rice field, road, house, tree, human being, flower, animal, stone or anything made out of stone. Interestingly, people who lack constituting ability will only sketch the ten objects side by side, while people with constituting ability spontaneously will sketch a landscape containing the ten objects.

In my experience, children in the lower grades of elementary school tend to sketch the objects side by side. As they enter the upper grades of the school, many gradually portray scenes. Although there is individual variation, it can be said that a person's constituting ability is developed by the time he or she is around ten years old. However a child who has a father who cannot act within a fixed framework, such as an alcoholic, continues to struggle in the upper grades. Even when they reach their thirties, such people may only be able to sketch objects side by side.

In our own daily lives this constituting ability is the skill to create some kind of order in life according to our own motives, values, and rules. In other words, it is the ability to voluntarily construct a fixed order or rule, on one's own, and to live by it.

This order or rule, or what I call "the sense of order" or "sense of rule," consists both of what is truly necessary for people to make their own lives in society and what is no longer necessary, which has become a bad custom that fetters and causes them to be unhappy. In this way, the constituting ability also involves the capability of distinguishing between what is necessary from what is unnecessary, of living according to what is beneficial, and of abolishing or improving what is useless.

Constituting ability also relates to the capacity to make judgements from a bird's-eye-view, to decide in which direction one must go, and to come up with large-scale strategic plans. For the individual, it is the capacity to lay out plans for one's life. In social terms, it is the capacity to foresee the course of history and to act as a guiding figure.

If this constituting ability is not developed, people will be unable to live according to the rules that are indispensable to a properly functioning society. An illustration of this in Japan is found in the recent fact that many students have begun to come late to class; in some schools the first period is continuously disturbed by students arriving late, one after another. Likewise, in my therapy practise, there has been a recent decline in the number of patients suffering from neuroses caused by an excessive straining of psycho-energy, and an increase in neuroses caused by a lack of mental ability, or rather by a lack of constituting ability.

Another important aspect of the Paternal Principle is the passing-on, and improvement (if necessary), of culture. By culture, I mean the mode and content of life on all levels, from the technique of making a living to the sense of moral and religious values. Passing on a culture is a kind of education. It is not an intellectual education, rather a "discipline" based on feeling which is put into practise in our daily lives. This means teaching the morals and standards common to society. If we consider this kind of education in the context of 19th century Europe, it was provided by the father who used his authority to compel and command. It not only arouses fear and forms the Super-Ego (*uber ich*), but works to create a pretense of one's own true self. This is what Freud calls the "Oedipus Complex." Thus, passing on a culture should not only depend on authority and compulsion; rather, it is preferable, to hand down a culture by having parents show good examples to their children. In order to make this latter kind of education possible, it is necessary for the father to always find some time to spend with his children.

As the time fathers spend with their children lessens, the more a child's constituting ability is likely to become deficient. Order will be lost, and the awareness of living according to rule, not to mention the awareness of the possibility of improving the rule (if necessary), will gradually diminish. If such a situation occurs, the child's desire to act according to what they feel at any particular moment will become so strong that their ability to maintain self-control will gradually deteriorate.

If the Paternal Principle is lost in society, the contemporary psychic current which values mental activity will gradually diminish, mental alertness will decline, morality will disintegrate, culture will no longer be passed down from one generation to the next, and only vulgar society will remain. The overall plans for society will be blurred, and the existence of society as a whole will be endangered.

On the other hand, if the Paternal Principle becomes too firm or solid, society will become authoritarian, mere convention will have great influence, individual creativity will be restricted, and society will become stagnant. capitalism helped emancipate the creativity of people who had been crushed by Feudalism. However, under expanding capitalism, the Paternal Principle has come to be viewed as something negative.

2. *The Paternal Principle and the Various Types of capitalism*

Although people sum up "capitalism" in one word, there are actually many types of capitalism. The first to appear was the capitalism of Western Europe, which gradually developed with the support of middle class producers and manufacturers, such as farmers and artisans. It was based on a local free market, rather than on an absolute monarchical government with a huge wholesale trading capital. In other words, this capitalism was based on free and independent individuals, supported by liberal ideas, and dependent on a free market.

The ideology of this capitalism was based on independent and liberal personalities. The notion that Liberalism has little to do with morality is a great misunderstanding, based on a faulty interpretation of Adam Smith's (1723-1790) liberal ideas. Smith, in his theory of "the Invisible Hand," emphasized that no matter how much an individual pursues profit, the general welfare will increase due to "the Invisible Hand." He does not say that a person can do anything in order to pursue profit. In fact he believed that a standard of maturity in personality was necessary for profit-making activities.

Smith's *An Inquiry into the Nature and Causes of the Wealth of Nations* appeared in 1776. Prior to this he had published a book entitled *theory of Moral Sentiments,* in 1759, which was in conversation with the "Moral Sense School" that appeared in England in the first half of the 18th century and carried out many studies on moral sentiments. In this latter work, Smith describes "benevolence" and "justice" as the basis of moral sentiments. But because he associated benevolence and justice with moral sentiments, liberal capitalism has been considered, by many people, as an ideal.

Even in areas of Western Europe where capitalism was not fully developed, ideas were developing that were central to the capitalism of the 18th century. In Prussia, Immanuel Kant (1724-1804) made *"Personlichkeit"* the final goal of practical morality; and in France, Jean-Jacques Rousseau (1712-1778) considered the innate feeling of *"pitie"* to be the basis of morality in human society.

In regions where classical capitalism was dominant, such as England, Holland, Southwest France, and the United States, there were many Protestants. In such countries, there was a great interest in a close appraisal of morality and personality. In other words, Protestant morality helped create the high moral standards of classical capitalism.

The point is that the cultivation of morality and personality is impossible without the Paternal Principle serving as a fixed constituting ability. It is crucial for enriching one's personality according to fixed values and standards, in planning one's life, and in accomplishing goals through the organizing of surrounding conditions by means of one's own abilities. The capability to do these things, that is, to have a personality that is independent and morally mature, is a prerequisite for a free market.

Compared to those countries which had a base of producers and manufacturers strong enough to allow the establishment of capitalism from the bottom up, countries which did not have such a base, i.e. Germany, Russia, Japan, China, etc., lagged behind in establishing it. Lacking the necessary base, these countries could not help but plan modernization from the top down as a giant national project. In Japan the State first created huge monopolistic enterprises, then sold them to private companies. Thus, capitalism in Japan started out from the very beginning as monopoly capitalism. Even marketing in Japan was placed under national control, to protect these monopolistic enterprises. There are many regulations in Japan today that continue to protect these monopolistic enterprises from free competition; and it is only since the present government came into office that the relaxation of regulations is being demanded for the first time. Countries slower than Japan in taking steps toward capitalism, especially those in Asia, consider Japan as their model and obviously follow its method.

When such a protective method of fostering capitalism is used, individual character and morals are considered as hindrances. Individuals are required to devote themselves to working as a part of their nation or society, and are not expected to be independent beings with their own powers of judgement. The ability to make moral judgements is discouraged, since it is said to disrupt "harmony," "peace," and "cooperation." For example, on Japanese school report cards, there is a section, separate from that used to note academic achievement, devoted to personality evaluation, and here "cooperative ability" is highly regarded. Furthermore, this "cooperativeness" is considered to be an important quality during entrance examinations for Japanese companies. In the interest of national capitalism, the concept of "personality" has been robbed of the spiritual aspect of morality, in favor of "cooperativeness." In other words, the concept of "personality" has been turned into a narrow-minded concept of "never taking a stand against others."

Property, which is prerequisite for personality, may exist as an entity in the legal system, but it does not exist in Japan in the dimensions of the reality of the senses. This is because property, which served as the basis for the classical capitalism of Western Europe, was something "proper" for the individual—that is, something with individuality. A concept of this kind has never existed within the tradition of national capitalism. In the world of middle-class producers and artisans who supported classical capitalism, property was never an abstract thing that was expressed only in terms of money. For example, a blacksmith's or carpenter's tools, or the field and pieces of agricultural equipment of the farmer, were things that were "proper" for certain individuals, and these things were precious to them. There was thus a fundamental connection between these "proper" things and "personality."

Under national capitalism, capitalists were capitalists and laborers were laborers from the beginning. What these people possessed was not proper individual property. The capitalists were possessors of abstract "capital," while laborers possessed only "labor." In such circumstances, there is no chance of developing a mental attitude which values personality and morality. The fact that Japan has a background of national capitalism explains why many Europeans find the Japanese to be the kind of people who are very good at working as members of an organization, but who have low moral standards as individuals, and whose enterprises, when considered as entities, lack a mature sense of morality.

Now, let us examine the development of capitalism in socialist countries, which undertook rapid modernization in the context of a planned economy. They failed to draw labor on a free and voluntary basis, and their economies, in spite of being considered by the socialists to be the most effective possible, collapsed, with the result that these countries are now looking to the free market as a way out of their predicament.

In ex-socialist countries like Russia and China, huge enterprises, that have until now been run by the State, are being sold to individual entrepreneurs. Thus, the establishment of capitalism, from the beginning, is being planned as a form of monopoly capitalism. Of course, individual property is also limited in these countries, along with the personality that is incident to it. In these societies, such factors have long been disallowed as being "petty bourgeois" and "reactionary." Thus, there is no sign of individual morality developing there. On the contrary, the dignity of the individual personality has not only been neglected but has also been placed under national supervision.

Although the free market is being introduced into these countries there is a decisive lack in the morality which serves as the basis for free market activities, in the barters and transactions; and as a result iniquity, bribery, and treachery are becoming a part of every day life. In addition, these countries are making very slow progress in the promulgation of the legislation necessary to establish impartiality, trust, and righteousness in the field of economic activity.

The problem of the underdevelopment of the personality and of its source, the the Paternal Principle, is clearly apparent in both the capitalism which grew out of national capitalism and that which grew out of socialism. The problem, however, does not end here. It further exacerbated by the great influence of the form of capitalism characteristic of today.

Although monopoly capitalism still exists, in the present age it has additional characteristics. That is, the system now depends on promoting large-scale consumption through the mass media; mass consumption is now the means of making profits. Under monopoly capitalism, monopolistic or oligopolistic enterprises made profits through the setting of high prices. Today these enterprises are shifting from a system in which they manipulated prices to one in which they manipulate public feelings and tastes through mass commercialization.

In a mass society, having one's own sense of values and individual feelings is being discouraged, while the number of people who blindly follow others without exercising their own will is increasing. The emphasis on "youth culture" further encourages movement toward a fickle and frivolous society. When this occurs, the Paternal Principle, which long supported self-control, prearranged life plans and self-discipline, becomes unnecessary, or even a nuisance, to be loathed by society.

The development of capitalism has always tended to weaken the concept of the Paternal Principle. As Alexander Mitscherlich pointed out in the 1960s, in a highly developed industrial society where the father goes to work outside of the home, his leadership at home is weakened. With the demise of the Paternal Principle people, estranged from traditional society and its values, are oriented to others, do not possess their own sense of values, and cannot help but become "momentary people," whose course of life is in a process of constant change. These people actually resemble a shoal of sardines, every one of them changing its course to go in the same direction as the entire group, swimming this way and that as if they were one great fish.

A good example of this "shoal-consciousness" is the recent history of Japanese tastes in dessert. There was once a time when the Italian dessert "tiramisu" was extremely popular; people soon lost interest in it and turned to Russia. Russian producers of lactic acid products benefited for a time; but the Japanese lost interest in this as well. The next fad, "natadecoco," came from the Philippines. Again this boom died away, with the result that a large stock of the dessert was left in the hands of the Philippine producers. People just follow trends, and when they lose interest in one, they move on to the next. Those who create the trends, form the tastes of society; and those who skillfully predict the upcoming trends, gain profit. In such a fickle mass society, individuality and personality become nuisances, and the Paternal Principle becomes the enemy, or something evil, which obstructs a lax and rule-free life-styles.

Japan's miraculous economic development has long been supported by two traits: the people's distinctive ability to suppress their individuality and work as part of an organization; and their non-individualistic ability to respond to new trends. From this perspective, it could be said that the Japanese are those best adapted to highly developed mass capitalism.

The shift toward mass consumption proceeds more smoothly in societies that have experienced national capitalism or socialism. Since those people have traditionally being uncritical and without principles, they can be freely controlled by commercialism. Societies that have experienced classical capitalism from the bottom up, where individual personalities and religious values prevail, are not so easily manipulated. In addition those people who desire a more humane life-style, cannot be driven to work long hours, all of which makes it more difficult for a consumption boom to occur. In terms of competitiveness, classical capitalism may be at a disadvantage in the future of mass capitalism, which is not say categorically that mass capitalism could not spread rapidly even in classical capitalist societies. Today, in Europe and the United States, young people since the 1960s have been inclined to praise such values as "kindness," "love," and "peace," rather than the the Paternal Principle.

The affluent society brought about by highly developed capitalism will no longer have a need for the Paternal Principle. In Japan many young people, even though they lack ascetic self-restoration, self-control, and the hard labor cultivated by the Paternal Principle, are nevertheless able to make a living doing temporary and simple-minded jobs (which the Japanese call "*arbaito*"—from the German "*Arbeit*"— or "part-time jobs"). These young people who do not have any regular or fixed jobs, and who lead carefree lives by doing whatever work they want, are called "freeters" in Japan. It seems as if people can go on living and society can continue without The Paternity Principle.

This, however, is an illusion. The fulfillment of the immediate needs of the existence of individual people may be possible, but the existence of an entire society, or of the whole human race on a global scale, is impossible without the Paternal Principle. Without the function of examining, judging, controlling, and guiding the direction in which the entire world is heading, the environment of the world will be destroyed, and the problems of war, food, and population control will remain unsolved. As a result the earth will probably end up in total chaos.

In a mass society, politicians are also chosen according to the standards prevalent in the society at large, and there is a constant danger of deterioration in the quality of those politicians. It is not only the mass society and its families who have lost the Paternal Principle; so have the politicians. As a result, colossal man-made and natural disasters will constantly threaten our society. The slow and incompetent response of the central and local governments to the huge earthquake in Kobe is something that should frighten us all, and it has been strongly criticized even within Japan. The unpreparedness was of course due as much to the government's irresponsible inability to plan effectively, as to the political ignorance and inability to take countermeasures for a predictable disaster. In other words, this was the result of the loss of the Paternal Principle.

The more a society appears to be coping successfully with mass capitalism, the more it advances towards moral corruption and chaos. The United States was the first society to take steps towards mass capitalism, and Japan was the next to follow. All countries that plan for economic development in the future will also follow the same steps. This means that a lack of the Paternal Principle will gradually become a worldwide problem.

3. The Paternal Principle and Changes in Family Structure

Looked at historically, the change in family structure has three aspects: the reduction in family size, the development of equality between husband and wife, and the loss of parental authority. These are all elements that encourage the decline of the Paternal Principle.

The reduction of family sized has, in general, gone along with the expansion of capitalism. In Europe this process had already begun under feudalism. In order to maximize the collection of land taxes, the feudal lord encouraged newly married couples to establish independent homes of their own. This "European marriage pattern" had been in practise since the Kingdom of the Franks in the 8th and 9th centuries. Data from the Carolingian era reveals that peasant families were predominantly nuclear families. Christian Europe, without a tradition of "ancestral veneration" to interfere, could easily center upon the mother and father of the nuclear family. In short, the tendency toward the equality of men and women was strong.

Viewed from the perspective of world history, the early establishment of the nuclear family in Europe is quite exceptional. In other parts of the world, large, complex families were dominant. In these "joint families," the married son lives with his parents along with several other married brothers. It is a structure in which families of the male line gather and live together, where the oldest male usually assumes the role of patriarchal leader, and descent is patrilineal.

This type of large family is the one most likely to collapse under the impact of the urbanization which accompanies the expansion of capitalism. Urbanization makes the younger generation, who live in the country, leave their aged parents and move to the city. As a result, the younger household in the city has no choice but to become a nuclear family. The spread of democracy and the concept of equality between men and women are other factors influencing the shape of a household which is not only independent from that of the parents, but devalues the authority of the parents, especially the father, and the elderly as well.

Accompanying this decline in the authority of the father is a crumbling of the sense of rule, the sense of righteousness, and the sense of justice, all of which have been maintained by the Paternal Principle. With the retreat of the Paternal Principle, the awareness of morality as a necessity diminishes. The good and necessary elements of traditional culture will no longer be passed on to succeeding generations, and the concern to determine whether a custom is good or bad, to improve or renew it, will disappear. The only thing that is likely to get stronger is the general denial of morality.

An incident which exemplifies this kind of problem occurred in Japan a few years ago. A female high school student in Kobe was killed by the iron gate of her school as it was being closed by a teacher. The background of this tragic incident is the fact that at this high school a large number of students had been coming late for the first period. Many steps were taken to get the students to come to class on time; nothing worked. The last step the school decided to take was one of force—to close the school gate when the first period began, so latecomers would not be able to enter the school grounds. Almost every morning a quarrelsome pushing of the school gate occurred. On one side were the teachers earnestly trying to close the school gate on time; on the other side were the students striving to get through the gate at the last second. On the day of the incident, a teacher was trying to close the gate with all his might, and the female student was the last trying to squeeze through the narrow opening. Unfortunately, her head was crushed by the school gate, and she died.

It must be recognized that the cause of this kind of horrible accident is the student's lack of awareness of order and self-control. A large number of students coming late to class is a symptom of this lack of self-control. That is to say, the parents of today's youngsters belong to a generation in which many negate the sense of values and order. This must be why a notable lack of self-control can be perceived in their children's generation.

Moreover, when considering this problem, the teachers did not try to clarify the defect psychologically and respond to it in an educational way. Instead they interpreted the tardiness of the students as a form of "laziness" and tried to correct it by force, by closing the school gate.

Behind this problem of students coming late to class lies the issue of the loss of the Paternal Principle. The incident in Kobe not only reflects a problem in Japanese society, but a growing, worldwide problem. The same problem came to light in the earthquake at Kobe. Despite the well-known scientific fact that there is no earthquake-free region in Japan, the people of Kobe and Osaka believed without a doubt that an earthquake would never occur in their area. The people's strong desire to believe that the land they lived on is good, is what allowed the fabrication of such a myth. Seismologists had warned them several times about the possibility of an earthquake; none of the residents, politicians, or bureaucrats took this warning seriously. The tragedy is that political leaders are not chosen for their abilities, rather for some other reason. On the whole, their blindness to the possibility of an earthquake in Kobe was due to an inability to make intellectual judgements or to guide; it can be said that it was due to a lack of the Paternal Principle.

One result of the loss of the Paternal Principle is that the bond of the family weakens. That is to say, the idea of "family diversity" will spread. For instance, many different forms of the "family" are develop-

ing: this can be seen in the spread of the nuclear family, the rising di-
vorce rate, children running away from home, the independence of
children, an increase in the number of unmarried people, and the emergence of "commuter marriages"—where the father has to live apart from
his family because of his transfer, the family cannot go with him because of difficulties in the children changing schools, the wife's job, or
parents to look after, etc.

In Japan there is now what is called the "hotel family." A comfortable life-style is guaranteed inside the home; however, the home is only
a place where the family returns to sleep. There is no emotional connection among the family members. It is a family without warm human
relationships. This type of dispersed family is the result of a lack of the
Paternal Principle; and, at the same time, the cause of it. Mass capitalist
society robs the family of its constituting and uniting abilities, making
the family diverse while also breaking up its warm human relationships, and causing the Paternal Principle to decline even further. It can
be said that the family, which is the fundamental forum of moral education, is now at the point of being dismantled, and that this dismantling
and the corruption of morality are closely interwoven.

4. The Paternal Principle and the Information Society

Mass capitalist society is also a highly developed information society. Mass consumption is created and maneuvered by the mass media
through commercials on television and advertisements in newspapers
and magazines. The aim of the mass media is to manipulate the senses,
tastes, and opinions of the general public. The degree to which the
general public is losing its ability to criticize and make independent
judgements is in proportion to its susceptibility to being influenced by
this mass media. New trends are constantly being created, and are soon
said to be out-of-date. A flimsy and frivolous culture of trends, often
called "youth culture," is thriving and gaining popularity.

Japan is unusual in today's world in allowing tobacco commercials
on television. Allured by attractive advertisements, many young Japanese have begun to smoke; indeed the number of smokers among the
young is increasing rapidly. Of course government policy and the laws

which allow the showing of tobacco commercials are important parts of the problem. But the young people who are easily influenced by the commercials and who lack the ability to make their own judgements, is of more concern. Behind this problem lies the issue of the absence of moral education in today's home.

It can be said up to now that the information industry has been used by mass capitalism to help stupefy the general public. The supply and manipulation of information has been the monopoly of the capitalists. The only opinions that could be disseminated were those in accord with the capitalists. An original opinion of one's own could only be addressed to a small audience.

Yet today the opportunity for small-scale communication is increasing. It is spreading through the practise of exchanging and receiving information by means of personal computers; if an individual's opinion is registered, anyone connected to the system can read that opinion. Even commercial suppliers, for a small fee, can gain access to the system if they choose. At present, this kind of information exchange is not as pervasive as television or the press, and its influence is small. Nevertheless, it is worth taking note of its principle. It is now possible for individuals to make their own choices about what is relevant in the flow of information and, rather than being passive recipients of a one-sided manipulation of information, to make their own use of the information.

The same could be said about the spread of cable television. This system allows residents of a certain district to create their own programs, with little capital outlay. Cable television allows individuals, or small groups of people, to become information or opinion suppliers, and there is a good possibility of a large number of people watching their programs.

The emergence of these new types of media effects both information suppliers and receivers. People will no longer be obliged to receive information that is of only one kind or fixed inclination. People will be able to choose on their own the kind of information they would like to receive. People will become capable of making their own judgements. Even people trapped within the sphere of socialism are now able to recognize the falseness and deceptiveness of the information which, up till now, has always been manipulated and controlled, so as to create a one-sided picture. Thus, the spread of television has caused a major social reform. Similarly, in capitalist societies, if it becomes possible for people to obtain information through different routes than those long dedicated to the one-sided manipulation of information, an improvement in people's ability to collect, arrange, examine, and judge information, might become a possibility. It would foster the discipline needed for people to make their own decisions.

In both politics and economics, the method of taking advantage of people by stupefying them arose from two sets of circumstances. Firstly, in the weakening of the Paternal Principle, people lost their ability to make their own judgements and to maintain self-control; and secondly, when the information being supplied to people was also being manipulated by the capitalists, the quality of the information did not allow people to judge properly. However society is likely to improve immensely if the following items become possible: the impossibility of the arbitrary manipulation of information; a sufficient supply of varying forms of information which were not previously available; and the acquisition by people of the ability to select relevant information from the variety of information obtainable. For something like this to occur, the return of the Paternal Principle would be essential, namely the constituting ability on both the levels of society and the individual. In order to improve the ability to make judgements on one's own, it can be said that there is an urgent need for the spread of moral education.

MIKIKO ISHII

THE THREE WITCHES IN *MACBETH*

In certain respects *Macbeth* reminds us of *Hamlet.* The heroes of both plays are incited to action by supernatural beings. But in *Macbeth,* the solemn majesty of the royal ghost in *Hamlet* is exchanged for the shapes of horror, dimly seen in the murky air, and revealed by the glare of the cauldron fire in the cavern. It is remarkable that almost all the scenes in *Macbeth,* the vision of the dagger, the murder of Duncan, the murder of Banquo, the sleepwalking of Lady Macbeth, and other scenes, take place at night or in some dark place. The sun shines only twice. First, in the scene when Duncan visits Macbeth's castle, around which the swallows are flitting, and Duncan ironically praises the castle of death: "This castle hath a pleasant seat; the air / Nimbly and sweetly recommends itself / Unto our gentle senses" (I. vi. 1-3). Secondly, it is daytime at the close of the play when the avenging army led by Malcom, a son of Duncan, wins the battle to regain the kingdom. The light of these two scenes casts the shadow of Macbeth's castle where an evil deed, a murder, is to occur.

The three witch characters of *Macbeth* are called "night's black agents" and play a formidable part in driving the hero to committing this evil deed. In the end, Macbeth realizes the truth about the witches, that is to say, their duplicity. In the cavern scene, he throws insulting words at them, "You secret, black and midnight hags!" (IV. I. 48). The breakdown of Lady Macbeth's own nature is marked by her sleepwalking scene. She is afraid of darkness and must have light by her constantly. The whole drama gives the impression that Shakespeare is delving into the dark side of the human soul.

The very first portrait of Macbeth that we have in the play is as a warlike hero. He is compared to the bridegroom of Bellona, the Goddess of War. Macbeth has just suppressed the rebellion of the Thane of Cawder, who supported the King of Norway's invasion of Scotland. Duncan, the King of Scotland, announces that in return he will bestow the title of the Thane of Cawder on "noble Macbeth". Duncan says, "No more that Thane of Cawder shall deceive / Our bosom interest. —Go pronounce his present death, / And with his former title greet Macbeth. / ...What he has lost, noble Macbeth hath won" (I. ii. 65-69).

However, the image of Macbeth as a noble warrior is immediately disrupted when Macbeth is greeted by the witches with three titles; Thane of Glamis which was inherited from his father, Thane of Cawder which he is going to receive, and future King. Banquo, Macbeth's fellow warrior, observes the sudden transformation of his noble partner.

> Good Sir, why do you start, and seem to fear
> Things that do sound so fair?
>   ...My noble partner
> You (the witches) greet with present grace, and great prediction
> Of noble having, and of royal hope,
> That he seems rapt withal. (I. iii. 53-57)

It is clear from this scene that something inside Macbeth is aroused by the witches. After the murder of Duncan, Macbeth is led from crime to crime to become a moral coward and a brutal murderer. Finally, he is called "this dead butcher" and his wife is called "his fiend-like Queen" (V. ix. 35). The noble Macbeth we meet in the beginning of the play is in stark contrast to this last image of "butcher". There is great difficulty in making the two contradicting images of the protagonist psychologically probable. Shakespeare creates a character with a strongly marked mixture of qualities. As A. P. Rossiter mentions, the "springs" of action of *Macbeth* are extremely mysterious:

> ...in *Macbeth* the springs of action are deeper, more mysterious and more alarming, because they seem so utterly beyond intelligent control, and so involved in the whole human scheme of things.[1]

This fall of grace from noble, warlike warrior to bloody butcher represents a profound and pathetic vision of evil. This vision highlights the interdependence of Macbeth's internal ambition on the one side and his openness to the temptations exerted by the witches on the other. We enter the mind of the protagonist and see the process of the brave hero who becomes a villain, and the view arouses our pity and terror. Without the witches, the irresistible tempters, the conflicting impressions we get of the hero could never be accepted as psychologically possible.

The prophecies of the witches are on the same level as the ghost's story in *Hamlet* or the poisonous lies of Iago in *Othello*. Macbeth is perfectly free to accept the prophecies of the witches or not. He is even more free than Hamlet is since the story told by the ghost of his father is more like an order to action than a prediction.

Through the relationship between Macbeth and the witches, Shakespeare tells us a truth about human nature: there is potential for evil in the virtuous, and for virtue in the evil. In *All's Well that Ends Well*, Shakespeare makes a comment on life: "The web of our life is of a mingled yarn, good and ill together; our virtues would be proud if our faults whipp'd them not, and our crimes would despair if they were not cherish'd by our virtues" (IV. iii. 68-71). Macbeth has something in common with the witches, but cannot completely free himself from the light of reason inherent in his character. His shadow is constantly exposed to this light, forcing him to face reality, which strikes his soul with the horror of his deed.

We are more or less ignorant of our natures, and do not know which path will lead us to happiness. According to W. C. Curry, Thomas Aquinas thought that every sinful act proceeds from an inordinate desire for some temporal good.[2] Macbeth is a noble warrior, but, obviously, has an inordinate ambition for a temporal good. Ambition is not itself dangerous or bad. It is his ambition which enables Macbeth to be a war hero, as is seen in the beginning of the play. But raw ambition divorced from the social norm is dangerous. The meeting with the witches on the heath is eventually fatal to Macbeth. They hail him with obscure suggestions. While Macbeth, who has just won the battle, instantly sees them in the context of his life, Banquo's attitude toward the witches is different. From the very beginning, he is doubtful about the witches. When he has heard their prophecies, Banquo asks them:

...I' th' name of truth,
Are ye fantastical, or that indeed
Which outwardly ye show? (I. iii. 52-54)

The moment the witches vanish from view, Banquo says to himself, "The earth hath bubbles, as the water has, / And these are of them" (I. iii. 79-80).

Macbeth is not driven to murder Duncan merely by the suggestion of the witches' prophesy. He has free will and freedom of choice. Whether to yield to their temptations or to resist them in his own responsibility. Whether Macbeth is predisposed to murdering Duncan before he meets the Witches has been a crucial point of discussion among critics. David Margolies thinks that a vision of murdering Duncan has already been present, though vaguely, in Macbeth's mind:

> In the light of the contradictions already internalized in Macbeth, the cause of his career of violence and Destruction can be seen to be present in himself. The Causal functions of the witches is to provide encouragement and confirm a vision that is already present, though vaguely, in Macbeth's mind. For the audience, they articulate the paradoxical quality of the play—"Fair is foul, and foul is fair." Their primary function is theatrical: they provide a spectacular element that makes a good show, which is symbolic and produces meaning in casting its eerie pall over the scenes and events that follow.[3]

H. B. Charlton, comparing Macbeth with Richard III, argues that Macbeth has sin in his soul, while Richard's energy is the strength of original sin.[4] We find a similar opinion in Williard Farnham:

> When the witches prophesy to Macbeth that he will be king, and thereby suggest to him the murder of Duncan, he clearly does not have an innocent mind. Banquo's question, why he starts at and seems to fear the words which sound so fair, can only mean that Macbeth has already entertained the thought of murder and because of it has already known the soul-shaking fear he later shows to his wife.[5]

Yet Kenneth Muir disagrees:

> Macbeth has not a predisposition to murder: he has merely an inordinate ambition that makes murder itself seem to be a lesser evil than failure to achieve the crown and so satisfy his wife. They both misjudge, destroying themselves for the sake of the other.[6]

Macbeth is ambitious. He is fallible and imperfect just like any other man, regardless of how brave he appears to be. Macbeth is rapt with the prophesies made by the witches, because they arouse his ambition. Unlike Banquo, Macbeth does not ask whether the witches are "fantastical" or not but immediately accepts them as real. What the witches have said is merely imaginary. Their knowledge is imperfect and uncertain. But this uncertain knowledge is transformed in Macbeth into reality. If we are to believe in the possibility of such a change taking place, we must be shown some signs of Macbeth's predisposition. The witches show their own knowledge of this. Let us look at the conversation of the witches in the opening scene on the heath.

> 1 Witch Where the place?
> 2 Witch Upon the heath.
> 3 Witch There meet with Macbeth. (I. i. 6-7)

After this conversation, they say in unison, "Fair is foul and foul is fair." We understand from this short scene that Macbeth has something in common with the witches. The witches' world, where "fair is foul and foul is fair" is a characteristic also inherent in Macbeth which is reflected in Macbeth's first speech, "So foul and fair a day I have not seen" (I. iii. 38). This is nothing but an echo of the witches' incantation. Macbeth instantly connects the witches' prophesies with his hidden ambition and is rapt with fantastical imagination. It is obvious that Macbeth, before he enters, has cast his shadow on the scene. What was hitherto only a possibility to Macbeth now turns out to be a reality. He cannot rise above his instincts, nor can he achieve rational understanding, because he refuses to question the true nature of the witches. His flaw is in accepting the witches, in whom his shadow is reflected, as perfection.

Macbeth greeted by the witches and he readily responds to them. "Thus Macbeth and Banquo, in effect, walk in the shadow of the witches once the prophesies have been uttered."[7] Lady Macbeth is well aware of her husband's dangerous personality. Her soliloquy proves that Macbeth has an inordinate ambition.

> Thou woudst be great;
> Art not without ambition, but without
> The illness that should attend it: what thou wouldst highly,
> That wouldst thou holily; wouldst not play false,
> And yet wrongly win; thou'dst have, great Glamis,
> That which cries, "Thus thou must do," if thou have it;
> And that which rather thou dost fear to do,
> Than wishest should be undone. (I. v.18-25)

In such a character as Macbeth, moral values are apt to be reversed. A greatness might be turned into a weakness. The higher he climbs the steps of glory, the more he is racked with feelings of guilt and conscience. In the speech quoted above, Lady Macbeth speaks of this streak in her husband without realizing it. The tragic debate of *Hamlet*, "to be, or not to be," is changed in *Macbeth* into "to do, or not to do." One voice within Macbeth cries, "You must act!" and another voice within urges him to do nothing. In his pursuit of kingship, Macbeth is viciously ambitious. Yet because of his fear of remorse, he is far from a simple villain like Iago or Richard III. His inner conflict between individualistic ambition and socialized attitude to the norm of the community makes Macbeth a more complicated hero than Hamlet and King Lear, and certainly than Othello. Macbeth is both good and bad in feeling and behavior. He has done one deed, and immediately repents what he has done. In the end, everything that he has done turns out to be as nothing, "a tale told by an idiot".

What Macbeth does get is the mockery which he always wanted. What seemed fair is, in fact, foul. In this recognition of his, there is something sublime pertaining to the virtue of the hero, although not heroic. The moment he meets the witches, Macbeth has sold his soul to them, but he cannot bring himself to submit entirely to them. He cannot get rid of his guilty fears. He is aware from the very beginning that the deed he contemplates is morally and socially evil, but cannot resist the temptation to achieve the crown.

Macbeth accepts the potential world of the witches, where normal order of nature is reversed, as is seen in their incantation, "Fair is foul and foul is fair." He admits that his ambition for the crown makes his hair stand on end and his heart knock against his ribs. Every word he speaks shows that he is struck to the soul with a realization of the horror of the murder. The light of reason inherent in him never fails to tell him that what he is doing is socially and morally wrong.

This realization makes him different from Shakespeare's other evil heroes such as King Claudius in *Hamlet* or Richard III. His partner, Lady Macbeth, never loses her sense of the difference between good and evil either. The couple choose evil to achieve a temporal good, and fall into a terrible moral dilemma. Lady Macbeth ends up racked by feelings of guilt, as is clear in her sleepwalking scene. The couple's actions bring home the moral that all the perfumes of Arabia will not sweeten the hands of the murderers.

Macbeth responds to the demonic power of the witches, but cannot completely give up his human nature. He cannot be a devil. This splits him in two. He is forced to live on two different levels, the level of the witches and that of human beings. This makes him see his real nature, the dark side of his personality. That is to say, he sees his shadow.

C. J. Sission, in his *Shakespeare's Tragic Justice*, warns modern psychologists not to take the witches, the ghost of Banquo in the banquet scene, and the dagger in the air as mere projections of Macbeth's mind.[8] But Charlton regards the witches as "impulses" familiar to human beings.[9] John Vyvyan remarks that they are nothing but psychic phenomena.[10] G. Wilson Knight, in *Shakespearean Tempest*, argues that the Weird Sisters are personified forces of disorder, disintegration, and conflict, hence, also, of tempest.[11] But there are other interpretations of the witches. C. J. Sission reminds us of the fact that Macbeth was played in the Jacobean Age. It was the age of the Scottish King, James I, who executed many witches for their evil powers and actions.

Today witches and witchcraft have almost been forgotten. Witches, as well as devils, are nothing but creatures of superstitions preserved in the history and records of the Church. When we hear the word "witch", our imagination conjures up an old woman in a fairy tale who flies through the air on a broomstick. But to Elizabethans and the Jacobeans, they were more significant and real. Most people believed that witches were channels through which the malignity of evil spirits might be visited upon human beings.

In *Macbeth*, the witches call themselves "the Weird Sisters" (I. iii. 32) and are called "the Weird Sisters" by Macbeth three times (I. v. 8; III. Vi. 132; IV. I. 136), and by Banquo twice (II. I. 20; III. I. 2). The word "weird" comes from "wurd" in old English, meaning goddesses subservient to Destiny, like Parcae in Roman mythology. There is an opinion that the Weird Sisters are Norns with great powers of destiny.[12] Norns, like Parcae, have the power to determine the past, govern the present, and foresee the future. They always appear in threes, and determine the past, present, and future of the people they meet. In *Macbeth*, the First Witch hails Macbeth with his past title, the Second Witch hails him with his present title, and the Third Witch foretells to him his future. In this respect they remind us of Parcae or Norns. However, the three witches in *Macbeth* have none of the divine elements inherent to goddesses or fates; for goddesses or fates usually have masters, and they do not need the chemistry or the cauldron fire to conjure up their powers. The witches in *Macbeth*, before they encounter Macbeth in Act IV scene I, prepare a boiling cauldron with the poisonous entrails of a toad, a snake or a frog. A. C. Bradley understands them as nothing but old women. He states:

> The witches…are not goddesses, or fates, or, in any way whatever, supernatural beings. They are old women, poor and ragged, skinny and hideous, full of vulgar spite…in accordance with the popular ideas, they have received from evil spirits certain supernatural powers.[13]

E. E. Stoll recognizes a correlation between the witches in *Macbeth* and the roles of devils in Christianity:

> They play both the roles…temptation and retribution…as do the devils in the Christian system: Nature itself, here no mere background, being in league with them. The immediate fulfillment of their prophesy that Glamis shall be Cawder, commented upon by the three who know of it, lends credibility to the other prophesies which ensue.[14]

W. C. Curry distinctly defines them as demons and devils in the guise of witches.[15] On the other hand, A. P. Rossiter is against this definition of the witches as devils. "They are not the Devil and therefore not in control of Macbeth, because they cannot move Banquo to evil, though they do stir up ill with him."[16] He also rejects the topical analogy between the Weird Sisters of *Macbeth* and the actual witches persecuted by the Church. "They are not the real or supposed witches that James tortured to the greater glory of God for they predict the future and predict it truly."[17]

The distinguished theory of Curry on the witches will show us a way to comprehend them from a philosophical point of view. As I have stated before, he thinks that the Weird Sisters are not witches but essentially demons and devils in the form of witches. He classifies the "astounding disorder" of demons or devils into firstly Neo-Platonic, and secondly Christian categories. Neo-Platonists conceived of the world as emanating from God through three successive spheres of activity, Rational Spirit, Universal Soul, and World Soul. God the Absolute throws light in the emanating world. Ultimate darkness in which the light of God loses itself is called "Matter." Matter is the opposite and negation of Spirit, therefore, evil. The word evil is not used here as something positively existent, but as a want or deficiency of good.[18] Demons, who are dwellers on the earth, exist between Matter and the Spirit World, and they were considered to be divine beings.

> Daemons may be said to represent the ultimate scattering forth of Spirit activities; are the lower order of divine beings whose sphere of activity is below the spiritual world...Daemons are, therefore, the necessary mediators between gods and men; they are divine beings who look upon the spiritual world, though they cannot inhabit it, and reveal its mysteries to human beings.[19]

However, Curry does not believe such a concept is at work in the witches of *Macbeth*. He notes the Christian point of view on witches; they are fallen angles cast out of heaven. All their natural powers which God bestowed on them remain unimpaired. They are still spiritual substances, though they are fallen. "Indeed, the function of demonic powers in the cosmic order is to participate in the working out of man's destiny."[20] Curry proposes the following characteristics of Christian demons:

1. They recognize and converse with one another through mental concepts, and upon these activities local distance places no restraints.

2. They are able to assume bodies of air, condensing it by virtue of their
   angelic natures, insofar as it is necessary for the forming of assumed
   bodies.

3. Everything that happens outwardly among men is known to them.

4. They know the future development of events conjecturally though
   not absolutely.

5. Their local movements from place to place are not on that account
   without purpose because they gain knowledge in order to act.

6. Nor are they subject to that "time" which is the measure of the
   movement of corporeal beings.

7. Demonic powers have the ability to move men's senses and imagination and will, sometimes to his destruction.

These characteristics of Christian demons are more or less found in
the witches of *Macbeth*. Can we then conclude that they are demons
according to Christian doctrine? The problem of the witches is not as
simple as it seems to be. *Macbeth* is a royal play performed in honor of
James I, when he welcomed the King of Norway, Christian IV, at his
court. King James was a Calvinist. He was very interested in witchcraft
and published *Daemonology* (1574) based on his experiences. He actually interviewed numerous witches and tried to find the cause of their
supernatural possession. Generally speaking, Scottish Calvinism em-
phasizes that the evil spirits who are the masters of witches are permitted
by God to exert evil in this world as part of the divine decree. They use
evil means to punish evil deeds. They are the instruments of Divine
Providence. In *The Royal Play of Macbeth*, Henry Paul distinguishes
between Scottish witches and British witches, and argues that *Shakespeare*
was greatly influenced by King James' treatises on Scottish witches.[21]
Scottish witches, like British witches, influence people by deceitful prophesies, under the instruction of devils, who have some knowledge of things
to come, but their oracular methods are more subtle than those of British witches.

Witchcraft was closely associated with sorcery, which cannot be considered without referring to heresy. In the old days, people believed that the world of light, good, and peace was eternally opposite to the world of darkness, evil, and strife. From the moment Christ was born, monism takes the place of dualism and becomes the essential principal of Western Philosophy. That is to say, the earth is combined with heaven through Christ and God becomes a man through Christ. This principle was systematized in scholastic philosophy around the end of the Middle Ages. On the other hand, various kinds of heresies appeared in Europe during the Middle Ages. Gnosticism, which was Manichaen in character, was rife throughout Medieval society and the Church. The Gnostic doctrine was originally based on Zoroaster. According to Montague Summers and others, those people who believed in Zoroaster assumed the existence of two original and independent powers of Good and Evil. Each of these powers was equal in strength, and supreme in its own dominion, while constant war was waged between the two.[22]

Gnostics were considered by the Church to be not only unbelievers who desecrated Christianity but also unnatural and antisocial and, therefore, menaces to society. But Gnosticism spread throughout Medieval society to an extraordinary degree. By the end of the thirteenth century, it disappeared, at least on the surface, due to severe condemnation by the Church. However, the idea that the Good and Evil powers were original, independent, and equal in strength persisted. The fact that execution of witches was rampant in England during the Jacobean Age suggests a close connection between Gnosticism and witchcraft.

A. C. Bradley comments on Shakespeare's sources of information for his play:

> Shakespeare took, as material for his purposes, the ideas about witchcraft that he found existing in people around him and in his books like Reginald Scot's Discovery (of Witchcraft) (1954). And he used these ideas without changing their substance at all.[23]

It must be noted that Reginald Scot remained skeptical about witchcraft. We do not know for sure whether Shakespeare agreed with James I's view of witchcraft or accepted the skeptical attitude of Reginald Scot. It is unlikely that Shakespeare adopted the scholastic position on witches in his play. Witches, devils, fates, and mere old women wrapped in rags are the various interpretations of Shakespearean scholars and the perpetuation of the debate itself demonstrates the elusive nature of the witches in *Macbeth*. They are traditional and tradition cannot be explained or examined by a set formula.

It is sensible to think that Shakespeare adopted the ideas about witches from those who were around him, including James I. But he never forgot to descend from the airy and imaginative realm of witchcraft to the firm ground of reality. Like Lady Macbeth or Banquo, the witches are important characters in the play. Their function is to stir up the half-conscious evil desire of Macbeth and to lead him astray by their ambiguous existence and by their half-true prophesies. Although they might have received certain supernatural powers from evil spirits, they are not "goddesses of destiny" or fates as are found in the *Chronicles* (1957) by R. Holinshed, which was Shakespeare's main source for the story of *Macbeth*. They tempt Macbeth only because they know his ambition to be king. In the same scene on the heath, the Third Witch hails him as what he shall be. Curry remarks on the ability of witches. "They know the future development of events conjecturally though not absolutely."[24] The witches seem to know the "seeds of time" but their suggestions are "nothing" to men because they are not subject to time which is the "the measure of the movement of corporeal things." They prophesy only what appears to be real. They are "imperfect speakers." They have only "strange intelligence," which evaporates as easily as breath into the wind or as bubbles in the water. What the witches have revealed to Macbeth is the world of momentary and impure unconsciousness. They have no power to compel Macbeth to rely on it. Macbeth is left free to accept the witches' oracles or to reject them. Their prophesy of the crown does not necessarily indicate evil means for achieving it. Macbeth might have achieved his ambition without murdering Duncan as he admits himself: "Chance may crown me / Without my stir." He feels he must take the responsibility himself for the first step to glory.

At the end of the opening scene, the witches say together, "Fair is foul, and foul is fair / Hover through the fog and filthy air" (I .i. 11-12). As I have already stated, Macbeth has within him the potential world of "fair is foul, and foul is fair." He knows that the witches are imperfect speakers as is clear in the scene where he calls to them. He says to them, "Stay, you imperfect speakers, tell me more" (I. iii. 70). He asks "the imperfect speakers" to tell him where they have got their "strange intelligence". In his letter to his wife, however, the word "imperfect" is changes into "perfect'st" and "strange intelligence" into "more than mortal knowledge" (I. V. 1-3). Macbeth plants an evil seed in himself in order to achieve his dream. He is condemned to self corruption because of his absolute belief in the witches.

Both Catholics and Protestants agreed that demons and devils could induce a man to sin by imaginative internal instigation. According to Thomas Aquinas, the interior part of the soul is intellective and sensitive, and the intellective part contains the intellect and the will, and therefore, the devil cannot instigate man to evil through his internal movements.

> Consequently, the whole interior operation of the devil seems to be confined to the imagination and the sensitive appetite, by moving either of which he can induce man to sin. For his operation may result in presenting certain forms to imagination; and he is also able to incite the sensitive appetite to some passion or other.[25]

Henry Paul also speaks of the extraordinary effect of the human imagination, linking it with the devil.

> ...a running comment put in the mouth of those who see them (the witches) constantly suggests that their awesome practices are due to hallucination of the beholder, very real subjectively, but objectively nonexistent...when Macbeth or Banquo sees them, the audience is kept aware that their doings and sayings are influenced by the imagination of those who see them, suggesting at once to the "judicious" that witchcraft may be but a delusion.[26]

Anton C. Pegis explains the idea of Thomas Aquinas about the devil that the devil can in no way compel a man to sin;[27] the sins of men are not entirely due to the devil's suggestion.

> Man was cast out of heaven on account of his rebellion against Gods will. Man, though he was originally endowed with perfection, caused his own degeneration by pitching his finite will against the infinite will. But he wins free will and freedom of action as a result. Thomas Aquinas argues that the

proper principle of a sinful action is the will, since every sin is voluntary, and consequently nothing can be directly the cause of sin except that which can move the will to act.[28]

Richard Hooker, an eminent English theologian in the Sixteenth century, speaks of the freedom of the will in his *Of the Laws of Ecclesiastical Polity,* published in 1593.

Man in perfection of nature being made according to the likeness of his maker resembleth Him also in the manner of working: so that whatsoever we work as men, the same we do wittingly we according to the manner of natural agents any way so tied, but that it is in out power to leave the things we do undone....There is in the will of man naturally freedom whereby it is apt to take or refuse any particular object whatever being presented unto it.[29]

A man is left free to decide for himself whether the instigation of the devils is real or imaginary. Macbeth and Banquo are introduced to the audience as brave warriors. Macbeth is praised as "Valor's minion", "valiant cousin", and "worthy gentleman". He is revered as a man who can act well and judge well. In the opening scene on the heath, after the witches have vanished, Ross and Angus, who are sent by Duncan, enter and announce to Macbeth that he has been made the Thane of Cawder. Banquo exclaims, "What! Can the Devil speak true?" (I. iii. 107). He realizes that the witches are real beings and the instrument of darkness. He advises Macbeth to beware of the witches: "That, trusted home, / Might yet enkindle you unto the crown, / Besides the Thane of Cawder. But 'tis strange: And oftentimes, to win us to our harm, / The instruments of darkness tell us truths; / Win us with honest trifles, to betray's / In deepest consequence" (I. iii. 120-126). Banquo doubts the prophecies of the witches, even though they have foretold that his descendants will be kings. But Macbeth does not cast doubt on their authority at all. Their "strange intelligence" only arouses his ambition and he is horrified with what he has discovered in himself. He says, "Present fears / are less than horrible imaginings. / My thought, whose murther yet but fantastical / Shakes so my single state of man" (I. iii 137-140). Through the contrast between Macbeth and Banquo, we know that witches or witchcraft have different meanings for different people.

Macbeth substitutes the fantastical for the real. His imaginative mind always obscures the distinction between the two. Before the battle with Macduff, Macbeth goes to see the witches in order to have oracular visions of the battle. He is told by the witches that he would never be defeated by a man born from a woman. At the battle with Macduff, Macbeth is told by him that he was born from his mother's womb untimely ripped. Macbeth realizes then for the first time that he has been deceived by the witches, and refuses to fight with Macduff. But it is too late to return to "this bank and shoal of time." He reaches for reality when everything has become irredeemable. He admits his failure when he realizes that he has destroyed his better part of man by relying in the witches' duplicity. Macbeth says then:

> Accursed be that tongue that tells me so,
> For it hath cow'd my better part of man:
> And be these juggling fiends so more believ'd
> That palter with us in a double sense;
> That keep the word of promise to our ear,
> And break it to our hope. (V. viii. 17-22)

Macbeth is inspired by the witches to murder Duncan and then encouraged by his wife to carry out the murder. Both the witches and Lady Macbeth know of Macbeth's inordinate ambition. The rest of his evil deeds, from the murder of the grooms to the murder of Banquo and the slaughter of Macduff's family, are driven by his neurotic fears born of guilt. These neurotic fears deprive Macbeth of nightly sleep. Lady Macbeth, too, is consumed with guilt. She is obsessed with the blood stains on her hands and the smell of the blood. She confesses their sins in sleep-walking, as if a second personality within herself speaks through her mouth. These are the outpourings of her repressed conscience. It might be thought that she suffers from demoniacal somnambulism.

The sleepwalking scene of Lady Macbeth evokes both great pity and terror from the audience. The scene is so poignant that it makes Bradley remark that, for the moment, all the language of poetry—even of Macbeth's poetry—seems to be touched with unreality, and this brief scene's toneless sentences seem the only voice of truth.[30] Lady Macbeth says:

> Out, damned spot! out, I say!—One; two:
> Why, then 'tis time to do't.—Hell is murky.—Fie,
> my lord, fie! a soldier, and afeared?—What need
> we fear who knows it, when none can call our power
> to accompt?—Yet who would have thought the old
> man to have had so much blood in him? (V. I. 33-38)

In contrast to Lady Macbeth, Macbeth never loses his senses. But he could not silence the voice from inside, that is to say, the light of his reason, which keeps crying, "Sleep no more." To those who have committed a crime, sleep is a place for the damned since sleep presents to them terrible visions and monstrous fancies which torment the miserable soul.

Supernatural beings like witches were natural beings to most of the original audiences of Shakespeare. We live in a time when very few believe in witches, demons, or devils, but this fact does not spoil our appreciation of the play. The witches and their doings are significant to us as symbols of the work of evil in the hearts of men. It is surprising that as early as 1603, George Gifford, a noted preacher of his time, wrote that the power of devils is "in the hearts of men, as to harden the heart, to blind the eyes of the mind, and from the lustes and concupiscences which are in them, to inflate them into wrath, malice, enuie, and cruell murthers: to puffe them up in pride, arrogance, and vain glorie: to intice them unto wantonness and the whooresomes, and all uncleannesse."[31]

The conversation of Macbeth with the witches and the phantom can be interpreted as simply the inner dialectical struggle of Macbeth with himself. The witches may symbolize the darker side of the character of Macbeth, his alter ego. The problem with such an interpretation is that the witches on their first appearance are seen and addressed by Banquo. Again Shakespeare refuses to give us a definite answer. But we need not be frustrated here, for C. G. Jung wrote, "A great work of art is like a dream, for all its apparent obviousness, it does not explain itself and is always ambiguous."[32]

The ghost of Banquo, which is seen only by Macbeth, might be a hallucination like the air-drawn dagger, caused by either Macbeth's frantic desire for security or by his guilt-stricken conscience. Macbeth calls the ghost of Banquo in the banquet scene "horrible shadow".

> If trembling I inhabit then, protest me
> The baby of a girl. Hence, horrible shadow!
> Unreal mock'ry, hence! (III. iv. 104-106)

When the assumed suicide of his wife is announced to Macbeth, he responds to it, saying, "There would have been a time for such a word." He articulates the pointlessness of his life and regards his whole life as a walking shadow cast by a brief candle.

> To-morrow, and to-morrow, and to-morrow,
> Creeps in this petty pace from day to day,
> To the last syllable of recorded time;
> And all our yesterdays have lighted fools
> The way to dusty death. Out, out, brief candle!
> Life's but a walking shadow; a poor player,
> That struts and frets his hour upon the stage,
> And then is heard no more: it is a tale
> Told by an idiot, full of sound and fury,
> Signifying nothing. (V. v. 19-28)

Both Macbeth and Lady Macbeth destroy themselves by selling their souls to the witches, and make their lives merely "a tale told by an idiot." In the end, Macbeth admits that his life is nothing but a walking shadow, signifying nothing, just like the ghost of Banquo, the air-drawn dagger, or the witches. Macbeth, by his own evil actions, has robbed his life of meaning. So his nihilism is the result of his crimes. His recognition that human life is a shadow cast by a brief candle extinguished in the dust of death, with all of its glories and splendors, and with its miseries and crimes, will leave behind an unforgettable moral lesson.

Notes

1   A. P. Rossiter, *Angel with Horns*, ed. Graham Storey (London: Longmans Green, 1961), p. 218.

2   See W. C. Curry, *Shakespeare's Philosophical Patterns* (Baton Rouge: Louisiana State UP, 1959), pp. 111-12.

3   David Margolies, *Monsters of the Deep: Social Dissolution in Shakespeare's Tragedies* (Manchester: Manchester UP, 1992), pp. 91-2.

4   H. B. Charlton, *Shakespearian Tragedy* (Cambridge UP, 1961), pp. 141-42.

5   Williard Farnham,. *Shakespeare's Tragic frontier: The World of His Final Tragedies* (Los Angeles: University of California, 1963), p. 106.

6   Kenneth Muir, ed. in *The Arden Edition of the Works of William Shakespeare* (London: Methuen, 1984), introduction, p. xlviii.

7   David Margolies, op. cit..

8   C. J. Sission, *Shakepearre's Tragic Justice* (London: Methuen, 1962), p. 13.

9   Charlton, op. cit., p. 160.

10 John Vyvyan, *Shakespearean Ethic* (London: Chatto & Windus, 1959), p. 15

11 G. Wilson Knight, *The Shakespearean Tempest* (London: Methuen, 1953), p. 188.

12 See the discussion in Muir, op. cit., introduction.

13 A. C. Bradley, *Shakespearean Tragedy* (London: Macmillan, 1964), p. 285.

14 E. E. Stoll, *Art and Artifice in Shakespeare: A Study in Dramatic Contrast and Illusion* (London: Methuen, 1963), p. 87.

15 Curry, op. cit., pp. 76.

16 Rossiter, op. cit., p. 220.

17 *Ibid.*, p. 220.

18 Curry, op. cit., p. 76.

19 *Ibid.*, pp. 64-65.

20 *Ibid.*, p. 72.

21 Henry N. Paul, *The Royal Play of Macbeth* (London: Macmillan, 1950), pp. 261-62.

22 Montague Summers. *The History of Witchcraft and Demonology* (London: Routledge & Kegan Paul, 1965).

23 Bradley, op. cit., p. 285.

24 Curry, op. cit., p. 74

25 *Basic Writings of Saint Thomas Aquinas*, ed. Anton C. Pegis (New York: Random House, 1944), vol. 2, p. 660.

26 Henry Paul, op. cit., p. 61.

27 Pegis, op. cit., p. 662.

28 *Ibid.*, pp. 259-60.

29 Richard Hooker, *Of the Laws of Ecclesiastical Polity*, ed. A. S. McGrade (London: Sidgwick & Jackson, 1975), pp. 122-24.

30 Bradley, op. cit., p. 400.

31 George Gifford, *A Dialogue Concerning Witches and Witchcrafts* (London, Printed for the Percy Society, 1842), pp. 22-3

32 *The Collected Works of C. G. Jung* (Princeton: Princeton UP, 1953-1977), vol. 15, p. 104.

JAY LIVERNOIS

THE SHADOW OF THE NOBLE SAVAGE

HEADHUNTING AND RITUAL CANNIBALISM IN SEVENTEENTH CENTURY NEW ENGLAND

1. Jean-Jacques Rousseau

Jean-Jacques Rousseau, the eighteenth century French Swiss philosopher, is the originator of not only the cult of nature and individual freedom but is also the inventor of the modern art of autobiography and political science as autobiography. In addition, through his scandalously personal *Confessions,* Rousseau was the first to claim a sexual identity and is, as a result, a much under recognized precursor of Freud and Freudian psychology. And through his proto-Romantic praise of the Alps, he started the fashion of visiting and touring Switzerland, and therefore it can be reasonably argued that Rousseau has been somewhat responsible for much of Switzerland's economic vitality over the last two centuries. But today, what Rousseau is best known for, particularly in North America, is his idea of the noble savage. In 1750 at the age of 38, he began to develop it in the following way.

Rousseau, while on his way to visit the French philosopher and encyclopedist Diderot (who was locked up in the notorious Vincennes prison), came across a notice of an essay contest sponsored by the Academy of Arts and Sciences of Dijon. The proposed subject by this Academy was: "Has the restoration of the arts and sciences had a purifying effect upon morals?" Initially Rousseau thought to argue that the revival of arts and sciences in European civilization had, yes indeed, improved morality. But he was not sure if he wanted to take up this rather common argument praising the wholesome effect of his contemporary culture and technology. Instead Rousseau thought he might argue something quite different and daring, namely, that no, morality had not improved with the development of civilization, and in fact morality was on a decline from the original "free" state in which savage humanity had begun in the primeval past. In Rousseau's alternative argument, the reason for this decline was that humanity was no longer free as it was in its savage original state, and due to the necessity in civilization of a binding social contract, "the arts, literature and the sciences…[just] fling garlands of flowers over the chains which weigh them [citizens] down."[1]

Still Rousseau was not sure which argument to use. He wrote both arguments down on paper and compared one against the other. Unable to make up his mind, he decided to ask Diderot for his advice while visiting him in prison. Diderot, much more intrigued by Rousseau's argument critical of civilization, persuaded Rousseau to take up this less conventional argument as he thought its unusualness had a better chance of winning the contest. Diderot was right, and with *A Discourse on the Moral Effects of the Arts and Sciences*, Rousseau won the first prize from the Academy of Dijon. Almost overnight Rousseau became famous not only in Dijon, but throughout France and Europe, along with the new ideas in his essay.

There are several peculiar, almost synchronistic twists and quirks in this story. One is how Rousseau was not sure which argument he wanted to use to compete for the Academy of Dijon's prize. Another is how Diderot's was the overriding voice that persuaded Rousseau to argue his unconventional and original ideas. Yet then another is that if Rousseau had not taken the argument he did, he might not have become famous and might have been at best just a minor figure in eighteenth century musicology, and therefore Rousseau's idea of the noble savage might easily have never come into existence.

But these oddities lead to more specific questions. First, did Rousseau have any particular "primitive" peoples in mind on which he based his ideas when he imagined his noble savage? Second, is Rousseau's idea of the noble savage totally original with him? And third, just what is Rousseau's idea of the noble savage?

In answer to the first question, the so-called "primitive" peoples Rousseau had in mind as his prototypes of the noble savage and to whom he refers in his work seem to have been the "Indians" in Brazil, the Caribs of the Caribbean, the Amerindians of French Canada and the Hotentots of South Africa. Rousseau knew about these savages from reading popular reports of travelers to the Americas and Africa. He first invokes the image of what he fantasized as these "free" savages in his attack on the commercial products of the arts and sciences in his prize winning essay, *Has the Restoration of the Arts and Sciences had a Purifying Effect upon Morals?* Rousseau sees the products of civilization as binding and enslaving, arguing that "They [Sovereigns] very well know that, besides nourishing that littleness of mind which is proper to slavery, the increase of artificial wants only binds so many more chains upon the people."[2] Rousseau's noble savage now makes its first appearance in his argument against the fruits of the newly restored arts and sciences, and he says: "The American savages, who go naked, and live entirely on the products of the chase, have been always impossible to subdue. What yoke, indeed, can be imposed on men who stand in need of nothing?"[3]

Secondly, the idea of the noble savage was not entirely original with Rousseau. It seems he derived it from a misreading of Montaigne's essay *Des cannibales*. Rousseau writes in a footnote in his prize winning essay:

> I dare not speak of those happy nations, who did not even know the name of many vices, which we find it difficult to suppress; the savages of America, whose simple and natural mode of government Montaigne preferred, without hesitation, not only to the laws of Plato, but to the most perfect visions of government philosophy can ever suggest. He cites many examples, striking for those who are capable of appreciating them. But, what of all that, says he, they can't run to a pair of breeches![4]

I say that this is a misreading of Montaigne's *Des cannibales* as the new historicist David Quint has argued decisively that Montaigne's essay is not about praising the cannibals of Brazil[5] but is a veiled criticism of 16th century France's Wars of Religion in general and the stoic Huguenots in particular (let us remember that Montaigne was a royalist Catholic).[6] And in fact it seems that Montaigne's claim that he received his anthropological knowledge about the cannibals of Brazil from a servant, on which he based his essay, is a fraud, and also his claim that he did not consult cosmographers for his information is a lie.[7] Out of this mix of fictions, Rousseau drew his inspiration for his idea of the utterly "free" savage.

But Rousseau only really developed his idea of the noble savage in *A Dissertation on the Origin and Foundation of the Inequality of Mankind*, which was his next submission to the Academy of Dijon after having won first prize in 1750. In this second discourse written five years later, which did not win a prize or even an honorable mention from the Academy, Rousseau more fully developed his fantasy of the "free" and noble savage. This more complete picture is where Rousseau's myth of the noble savage comes together and is really fleshed out.

Rousseau first mentions "the savages" in this essay as an *exemplum* of natural health in his scathing criticisms of medicine as it was practiced in his day. He claims that most diseases are caused by civilization and its resulting medicine, "and that we might have avoided them nearly all by adhering to that simple, uniform, and solitary manner of life which nature prescribed."[8] Rousseau imagines that his own tendency to be a recluse is an *a priori* condition of nature and the first principle of existence in the primeval state, and that isolation from society means health. Rousseau says:

> When we think of the good constitution of the savages, at least of those whom we have not ruined with our spirituous liquors, and reflect that they are troubled with hardly any disorders, save wounds and old age, we are tempted to believe that, in following the history of civil society, we shall be telling also that of human sickness.[9]

Rousseau, a Swiss, thinks that primitive people are never ill, so he concludes they must not have any medicines. He says: "Being subject therefore to so few causes of sickness, man, in the state of nature, can have no need of remedies, and still less of physicians:"[10] Therefore the first component of Rousseau's noble savage is a human who is never ill and who has no need of medicine because they live in a perfect, natural state; an Ur-Eden.

Physically Rousseau imagines the noble savage as having highly developed senses like wild animals, because for Rousseau, people in nature are "solitary, indolent, and perpetually accompanied by danger...."[11] As a result Rousseau thinks that primitive people have highly developed and, when compared to degenerate, civilized people, almost supernatural senses. Rousseau points out that:

> It is therefore no matter for surprise that the Hottentots of the Cape of Good Hope distinguish ships at sea, with the naked eye, at as great a distance as the Dutch can do with their telescopes; or that the savages of America should trace the Spaniards, by their smell, as well as the best dogs could have done; or that these barbarous peoples feel no pain in going naked, or that they use large quantities of pimento with their food, and drink the strongest European liquors like water.[12]

In fact Rousseau's noble savage is seen as being basically animal and blissfully unconscious. He says of his savage:

> The only goods he recognizes in the universe are food, a female, and sleep: the only evils he fears are pain and hunger. I say pain, and not death: for no animal can know what it is to die; the knowledge of death and its terrors being one of the first acquisitions made by man in departing from an animal state.[13]

And when it comes to reflection, Rousseau says,

> It would be melancholy, were we forced to admit that this distinctive and almost unlimited faculty is the source of all human misfortunes; that it is this which, in time, draws man out of his original state, in which he would have spent his days insensibly in peace and innocence;[14]

And Rousseau's primitive is also the naive existentialist. He says that:

> His soul, which nothing disturbs, is wholly wrapped up in the feeling of its present existence, without any idea of the future, however near at hand; while his projects, as limited as his views, hardly extend to the close of day. Such, even at present, is the extent of the native Caribbean's foresight: he will improvidently sell you his cottonbed in the morning, and come crying in the evening to buy it again, not having foreseen he would want it again the next night.[15]

Another aspect of Rousseau's noble primitives is that they are not suicidal. Rousseau juxtaposes his fantasy of primeval existence with life in eighteenth century Europe where, according to him, people are miserable, suffer from despair and lean towards suicide. Rousseau says,

> We hardly see anyone around us except people who are complaining of their existence; many even deprive themselves of it if they can and all divine and human laws put together can hardly put a stop to this disorder. I would like to know if anyone has heard of a savage who took it into his head, when he was free, to complain of life and to kill himself. Let us be less arrogant, then, when we judge on which side real misery is found. Nothing, on the other hand, could be more miserable than a savage exposed to the dazzling light of our 'civilization', tormented by our passions and reasoning about a state different from his own.[16]

Of course imbedded in this fantasy is Rousseau, the recluse who *"hates the dazzling light of our 'civilization'"* and desperately wants to be "free" of it. He projects this desire for freedom onto his fantasy image of the savage. But one of the most surprising elements of Rousseau's noble savage is the incredible assertion that the primitive is not violent. Rousseau comes to this conclusion because he believes that primitive people do not have any possessions to fight over so "Their quarrels therefore would seldom have very bloody consequences; for the subject of them would be merely the question of subsistence." He also thinks that primitive people are not very passionate as "The imagination, which causes such ravages among us, never speaks to the heart of savages, who quietly await the impulses of nature, yield to them involuntarily, with more pleasure than ardour, and, their wants once satisfied, lose the desire."[17] He then reasons:

> And it is the more absurd to represent savages as continually cutting one another's throats to indulge their brutality, because this opinion is directly contrary to experience; the Caribbeans, who have as yet least of all deviated from the state of nature, being in fact the most peaceable of people in their amours, and the least subject to jealousy, though they live in a hot climate which seems always to inflame the passions.[18]

Rousseau reaffirms this non-violent portrait of the noble savage by saying:

> Let us conclude then that man in a state of nature, wandering up and down the forests, without industry, without speech, and without home, an equal stranger to war and to all ties, neither standing in need of his fellow-creatures nor having any desire to hurt them, and perhaps even not distinguishing them one from another.[19]

This image of the primitive is based almost totally on Rousseau's fantasy. He provides no real examples or proofs for imagining Neolithic people as non-violent; he simply makes it up.

The problem with this wonderful fantasy of primitive humanity is that not only is it false, but since the debut of Romanticism at the end of the eighteenth century, this fiction has dominated how both past and present Neolithic cultures are seen by us. This paradigm has influenced our culture's sense of ourselves, as it has obscured our past, and it has blocked our understanding and appreciation of the primitive other. This fiction, this reclusive and solitary fantasy of the primitive, through movies, books, anthropology, art, New Age psychologies and therapies, and politics, has skewed the way we understand ourselves today. Our culture, Neolithic culture and even our savage dreams as they often stalk us at night are still at stake. So let us now look at the shadow of this noble, passionless, non-violent, solitary primitive, something that Rousseau never considered. After all, if you were trying to create the noble savage, why would you want to say anything ignoble about him?

2. Headhunting and Cannibalism in 17th Century New England

Roger Williams, the dissident Puritan minister who was the first great American advocate for the idea of the separation of Church and State, and who also was the founder of Providence, Rhode Island, put together while sailing from the Dutch colony of New Amsterdam (what is now New York) to England, *A Key into the Language of America.* Written in 1643, this is one of the earliest works on America and is not only a rudimentary dictionary of a Native American language, the Narragansett's, but is also an extensive commentary on New England's indigenous culture. New England was inhabited at this time of European contact and colonization by the Algonquin or Eastern Woodland tribes, of whom the Narragansett were a large and important group located in southern New England around what is still called Narragansett Bay.

A Key into the Language of America is not organized in a lexicographic format but is structured chapter by chapter as a history of the Narragansetts "from their Birth to their Burialls."[20] This results in Williams presenting, along with the Narragansett vocabulary, a descriptive critique of their culture and lifestyle. In the body of the text, Williams contrasts this "American" life and culture to the life led by English colonists of New England and the so-called "degenerated"[21] culture of England which the Puritans had left.

On reading through *A Key*, in Chapter VII, titled "Of their Persons and parts of body," I came upon the following gloss which stunned me. "The Mauquauogs, or Men-eaters, that live two or three [hundred] miles West from us, make a delicious monstrous dish of the head and brains of their enemies;"[22] The tribe that this passage refers to is the Mohawk of the Iroquois confederation who were located in what is now the state of New York. The Mohawks had a fierce warrior reputation, and in the seventeenth century they often raided well into southern New England. They would scream and boast when attacking their enemies, "We are the Mohawks, we will eat your hearts and drink your blood." I had never read or heard that they had literally carried out these rather bloody acts of cannibalism and terror. I had always thought the Mohawk warriors yelled this to throw panic into their enemies. On first reading this information I dismissed it. It simply seemed that the Narragansetts were disparaging their foes by attributing to them monstrous deeds and habits.

Yet reading on in *A Key*, I was further surprised to find the following:

> Timequássin *To cut off*, or *behead*, which they are most skilful to doe in fight: for, when ever they wound, and their arrow sticks in the body of their enemie, they (if they be valourous, and possibly may) they follow their arrow, and falling upon the person wounded, and tearing his head a little aside by his Locke, they in the twinkling of an eye fetch off his head though but with a sorry knife.[23]

This was another thing I had never heard of before. Nowhere is it written in the histories of New England that the indigenous people deliberately cut off the heads of their enemies in battle which would mean that they were headhunters. The practice of Indians scalping is well-known, but even that has been attributed to the brutal influence of Europeans paying a bounty to so-called "friendly Indians" for the deaths of "unfriendly Indians," with the scalps being the proof for payment. From this point on, I began to read *A Key* more closely for any other glosses on the Narragansetts' headhunting practices. In it I found the following:

> *Ob.* They are much delighted after batell to hang up the hands and heads of their enemies:[24]

> ...and yet having no Swords, nor Guns, all that are slaine are commonly slain with Great Valour and courage: for the conquerour ventures into the thickest, and brings away the Head of his Enemy.[25]

> though sometimes the *Sachim* sends a secret Executioner, one of his chiefest Warriours to fetch of a head, by some sudden unexpected blow of a Hatchet, when they have feared Mutiny by publike execution.[26]

Fascinated by these further proofs, I began to scour all the contemporary works on New England's Native American culture, history, and their warrior customs. There was almost no mention of headhunting except for a sentence on the results of a battle that occurred in northern New England between the Algonquin tribes of the Micmac and Abenaki in 1607. "And the victors celebrated their triumph in traditional fashion, returning with the heads of their dead enemies plus live prisoners for torture."[27] The Native American custom of the ritual torture of prisoners is well known if now somewhat lost in a kind of amnesia brought on by the revisionist politics of correctness and multiculturalism, but again here is a clear reference to the cutting off the heads of enemies and bringing them back as trophies, and it is clearly stated that this was "traditional custom."

I next examined nineteenth century and earlier accounts of New England's Native American history to find if there was any more proof of headhunting habits. I was able to find a verbatim account of a conflict between rival tribes in a coastal area just south of Narragansett territory in 1654.

> A number of Pequots…set out one day in search of Ninigret's camp, with the intention of obtaining an interview with their kindred there and persuading them to desert the Nehantics. They were met in the forests by three of Ninigret's Pequots, who demanded of them what they were doing there. "O! we have some things to do," was the answer. "How many are there of you?" "Thirty." "Then there are thirty heads for us," fiercely responded the three boasters. "but we are in the employ of the English: we carry burdens or letters where they wish to send them." "We will have those thirty heads before to-morrow afternoon in spite of the English," replied the strangers;[28]

Here, again, and word for word, the Indians are looking to take heads.

I found another account supporting a headhunting thesis in a description of the Mohegan *sachem* Uncas (the Mohegans were a neighboring tribe of the Narragansetts), triumphing in a fight and his subsequent actions. "Uncas shot the chief with an arrow, cut off his head, and stuck it up in the crotch of a large oak, where the ghastly trophy remained withering and bleaching for many years."[29] This is certainly headhunting at its finest.

But in searching for more evidence that New England's seventeenth century Neolithic warriors were engaged in headhunting, I also came upon accounts of Native Americans involved in what seems to have been ritual, and definitely not subsistence, cannibalism. The following is a relation of how the Mohegans in their customary fashion dealt with a traitor captured during the Pequot War.

> Uncas claimed the right to execute this Indian after the custom of his tribe. Never was justice meted out to a wretch with a more lavish hand. He was torn limb from limb, and roasted in a fire kindled for that purpose, and then passed around the council-ring, and eaten by Uncas and his Mohegans with a relish equaled only by the demonstrations of joy with which they threw the bones into the fire when they had completed their meal.[30]

Next is the gruesome account of the notorious execution of the captured Narragansett *sachem*, Miantinomo, by Uncas and his brother.

Uncas repaired to Hartford, took the captive into his custody, and, accompanied by a file of English soldiers, who were sent to protect him from the vengeance of the Narragansetts, proceeded to execute the warrant. Two other Englishmen were also sent to remain by the prisoner, and see that no barbarities were practiced at the execution. Uncas took Miantinomoh, and led him to the place where he had been taken. When they had reached the fatal spot, the brother of Uncas, who was marching behind Miantinomoh, split his head with a hatchet and killed him at a blow.

Notwithstanding the presence of the two Englishmen, Uncas cut a piece from the shoulder of his fallen enemy, and ate it in savage exultation. "It was the sweetest meat he ever ate," he said, and added complacently, that "it made his heart strong."[31]

There is even mention of cannibalism among Indians found in the reports from a Vatican official traveling through New England late in this period. Niccolo' Forteguerri, secretary of Propaganda for the Holy Roman Catholic Church, wrote in 1709 that the Indians of New England had reverted back to their traditional role of being "fond of eating human flesh,"[32] and again I want to emphasize the word traditional.

From these accounts it seems that New England's seventeenth century Native Americans were customary and traditional headhunters and cannibals. But slowly through the post-contact period, as they assimilated more and more into English colonial culture and as European technology changed their lifestyle, New England's Indians gave up the practices of headhunting and cannibalism along with their polytheistic religion. Yet several questions come up if these accounts are reliable. For example, why has so little note been taken of these practices? Why was no attention paid to them among the English writers of that time? And what perhaps did the actions and rituals of war religiously mean to the Neolithic people practicing them?

3. Headhunting and the Algonquin Soul

It seems that seventeenth century English writers were not shocked or horrified by the headhunting of New England's aborigines because, it should be remembered, the English themselves were accustomed to decapitation. The seventeenth century New England Puritans especially were not about to be offended by the practice of detaching heads from bodies, after all their co-religionists in England cut off the head of King Charles I. In fact when administering capital punishment to Native Americans, the English colonists routinely cut off Indian heads and put them on display in public places rather than hanging the individuals. Here is one example of an Indian encounter with English capital punishment.

> …The townsmen were enabled to recognize in him a fellow named Busheag. With a great deal of difficulty the Indians were persuaded to surrender him; he was carried to New Haven, tried for his crime, convicted and sentenced to decapitation. Busheag sat erect and motionless, while the unskillful executioner mangled him with eight blows upon the neck, before he could detach the head from the body. This execution seems to have satisfied both parties; the Indians became tranquil, and the English do not appear to have made any further demands for the murderer of the servant.[33]

Capital punishment was used on Indians in all the colonies especially in Pilgrim Plymouth and Puritan Boston. Besides, the English, like the Algonquins, also demanded or took heads as signs of victory in war.

The whites responded:

> "This excuse will not serve. We know well that it is not true. You must give us the heads of those who have slain our people, or we will fight with you."[34]

> He [Canonchet, chief of the Narragansetts during King Philip's War] was carried to Stonington, and there executed in such a manner as would give each tribe of warriors who were with Denison [an English officer] a share in

the deed…. Cassainamon's men shot the devoted *sachem*; the Mohegans
beheaded and quartered him; the warriors of Catapazet kindled the fire on
which his body was burned. His head was preserved by Denison as a trophy,
and was sent to the magistrates of the colony.[35]

Another reason that not much is made of the headhunting practices
of New England's Neolithic people is that most of the contemporary
accounts about them were written by missionaries who wanted to portray Indians in the best light possible. This was done so that people in
England would continue to send money to convert the native pagans to
the English God. John Eliot, the famous "Apostle to the Indians," in all
his many books on his years of missionary experience with New England's
Native Americans, never once remarks about headhunting or cannibalism. It was not in his financial interest to do so. It seems the English
were much more horrified and fascinated by the Indian warrior custom
of torturing prisoners to death and the delight Indian women and children took in this "sport."

Another reason these indigenous customs were not widely remarked
on or written about was that the Puritans had an aversion to learning
anything about their pagan neighbors. The Puritans were deathly afraid
that they might become contaminated by the local heathens and, with
what seemed to them, their lazy and sinful life. In fact this did indeed
happen as many traders and friends of the Indians, like Thomas Underhill,
Major Fitch and James Perrin, were so deeply influenced by Native Americans and their sense of freedom, that they permanently moved out of the
controlling environment of Puritan culture.

Still the question remains, why were the New England Indians headhunters? The answer seems to lie in Williams' *A Key*. Williams writes:

> Wuttìp.   *The braine.*
> *Ob.* In the braine their opinion is, that the soule (of which we shall speake in
> the Chapter on *Religion*) keeps her chiefe seat and residence:[36]

The belief that the soul of a person is located in the brain is common among Neolithic cultures. For example the Asmat people of Irian
Jaya, which is the western half of New Guinea and part of Indonesia,
believe that a newborn does not have a soul until a head is cut off in a

raid and given to the child. The head is stripped of flesh, dried, carved and decorated. It is then used as a pillow for the rest of the person's life and acts as a dream vehicle for the soul.

The Native Americans of New England seem to have had a variation of this belief but split in two. This soul dualism is in Williams' *A Key* under the Chapter on religion. He writes:

> Cowwéwonck.   *The Soule,*
>> Derived from *Cowwene* to sleep, because say they, it workes and operaates when the body sleepes. *Michachunck* the soule, in a higher notion, which is of affinity, with a word signifying a looking glasse, or cleere resemblance, so that it hath its name from a cleere sight or discerning, which indeed seemes very well to suit with the nature of it.[37]

One of the souls here is associated with sleep and is a ghost soul, while the other is connected with intelligence. Both of these souls were located in the brain for native New Englanders, but they could become split off especially after a violent death.[38] Then the dream soul would wander and cause all kinds of sickness and create all kinds of misfortunes.

This belief in a wandering, evil ghost is found throughout the world and is probably a remnant of Neolithic shamanic religion. It seems to be referred to even in the sophisticated, Chinese oracle *I Ching* in the definition of one of its aspects for "Adversity, *LI:* poisonous, sinister, cruel, contrary. It indicates a spirit or ghost that seeks revenge by inflicting suffering upon the living. Pacifying or exorcizing such a spirit can have a healing effect."[39]

It is my belief that the New England Algonquins of the seventeenth century took enemy heads in order to not only insure the death of their victims but also to capture the two souls of the dead and most particularly the ghost or dream soul. The Indians, having a special fear of the ghosts of the dead, by cutting off an enemy's head and hanging it in lodge, insured power over a potentially vindictive ghost/soul. Oddly enough for us, they slept better with human heads hanging around them.

It is also my belief that New England's Native Americans occasionally ate individuals to ingest the power of their victims. It seems that to be eaten by them meant having special qualities, possessing or being possessed by *manitou,* a god. That's why Uncas relished eating part of his great Narragansett rival, Miantinomo, after executing him, and "it made his heart strong."

Still it does not make sense that the headhunting and ritual cannibalism of New England's indigenous tribes in the seventeenth century is not better known. Not only is it not known, but it is also never discussed or written on. I believe the reason for this is the glowing image of the noble savage we get from Jean-Jacques Rousseau. This romantic image of the natural, non-violent, solitary human has almost no (what we would call today) darkness or shadow as Rousseau invented this creature in the eighteenth century out of his "perfect" imagination. When we imagine Native Americans, and now probably all indigenous peoples throughout the world, we do not, we cannot see this darkness, this *other*, unsavory aspect of the noble savage. What we do see is an almost shadowless Romantic fiction. This fiction has distorted what I believe is a truer image of the Native American in seventeenth century New England—a splendid Neolithic headhunter and cannibal but with a polytheistic sensibility and soul.

Notes

1   Jean-Jacques Rousseau, *The Social Contract and Discourses*, tr. G. D. H. Cole (Vermont: Charles Tuttle, 1993), pp. 4-5. It was this idea of European civilization predicated on a "social contract," unhappily limiting individual freedom, that occupied Rousseau's thinking almost to the end of his life, and from the beginning this line of thought devolved from his fantasy of a prior "free" savage state of humanity.

2   *Ibid.*, p. 5.

3   *Ibid.*, p. 5.

4   *Ibid.*, fn 5.

5   David Quint, "A Reconsideration of Montaigne's *Des cannibales*," *America in European Consciousness: 1493-1750*, ed. Karen Ordahl Kupperman (Chapel Hill: North Carolina Press, 1985), (fn) p. 188.

6   *Ibid.*, pp. 166-191.

7   *Ibid.*, p. 168.

8   Rousseau, p. 56.

9   *Ibid.*, p. 56.

10   *Ibid.*, p. 57.

11   *Ibid.*, p. 58.

12   *Ibid.*, p. 59.

13   *Ibid.*, p. 61.

14   *Ibid.*, p. 60.

15   *Ibid.*, p. 62. Clearly, Rousseau, and the traveler who relates this information, did not understand the complex nature of the exchange system practised among Native Americans. Hence the origin of the pejorative label of "Indian giver" for someone who gives gifts and then takes them back.

16   *Ibid.*, pp. 70-71.

17   *Ibid.*, p. 78.

18   *Ibid.*

19   *Ibid.*, p. 79.

20   Roger Williams, *A Key into the Language of America*, ed. John J. Teunissen and Evelyn J. Hinz (Detroit: Wayne State UP, 1973), p. 36.

21   *Ibid.*, p. 130.

22   *Ibid.*

23   *Ibid.*, p. 131.

24   *Ibid.*, p. 132.

25   *Ibid.*, p. 237.

26   *Ibid.*, p. 203.

27   Neal Salisbury, *Manitou and Providence: Indians, Europeans, and the Making of New England, 1500-1643* (New York: Oxford UP, 1982), p. 71.

28   John W. De Forest, *History of the Indians of Connecticut* (Hartford: Hamersley, 1851), p. 245.

29   De Forest, p. 145.

30   G. H. Hollister, *The History of Connecticut*, vol. I (Hartford: L. Stebbin & Co., 1858), p. 55.

31   *Ibid.*, pp. 123-24.

32   In Italian Forteguerri writes: *"vaghi di mangiare carne umana...dotati di gran froza ed altissimi di statura; di religione idolatri."* Luca Codignola, "The Holy See and the Conversion of the Indians," *America in European Consciousness*, ed. Karen Ordahl Kupperman, (Chapel Hill: North Carolina Press, 1995), p. 214, (fn) 238.

33   De Forest, p. 210.

34   De Forest, p. 97.

35   *Ibid.*, p. 283.

36 *A Key*, p. 130.

37 *Ibid.*, pp. 193-94.

38 Åke Hultkrantz, *Conceptions of the Soul Among North American Indians* (Stockholm: The Ethnographical Museum of Sweden, 1953), pp. 73-114.

39 *I Ching*, tr. Rudolf Ritsema and Stephen Karcher (Ascona, Switz.: Eranos Foundation, 1995), pp. 663-64.

CLAUDIO RISÉ

THE DARK SIDE OF PSYCHOANALYSIS

Psychoanalysis from the beginning chose to deal with the dark side of humanity. The founders of the analysis of the unconscious were fully aware of the morbid and dangerous stuff they were presenting to the world. Sigmund Freud, commenting to fellow analysts C. G. Jung and Sandor Ferenczi, about the enthusiasm of the American people waiting for their visit, said, "They don't know we are carrying a plague to them."[1]

So the dark, the "*Acheronte movebo*" is, for Freud and Jung, the very color of the analytical experience. It guarantees the analysis a disturbing atmosphere; this "*unheimlich*" quality is inherent to transformation. As Jung said, speaking on Freud's discoveries;

> "Indeed it is a frightening thought that man also has a shadow side to him, consisting not just of little weaknesses and foibles, but of a positively demonic dynamism... A dim premonition tells us that we cannot be whole without this negative side, that we have a body which, like all bodies, casts a shadow, and that if we deny this body we cease to be three-dimensional and become flat without substance. Yet this body is a beast with a beast's soul, an organism that gives unquestionable obedience to the instinct. To unite oneself with this shadow is to say yes to the instinct, to that formidable dynamism lurking in the background...has anyone made clear to himself what that means, a yea-saying to instinct."[2]

Since analysis moves in the dark waters of the Acheronte, bravely meeting our own shadow and facing the darkness of our own instinct, then the dark side of analysis, its shadow, manifests itself precisely in the denial of its darkness.

The denial of shadow usually begins in adolescence, in this case, in the adolescence of psychoanalysis. In the infancy of psychoanalysis Freud, its father, dared to recognize that "in his most deep essence man is made by elementary drives," and opposed the erotic drives (relating to sex) with the ego drives of survival and hunger (relating to power).[3] Later on, in the adolescence of the movement, this view changed considerably. Apparently the experience of the First World War, which in the beginning Freud looked upon with enthusiasm,[4] contributed to a more "educated" attitude.

Facing the disastrous effects of the war Freud desperately tried to comprehend "the brutality that single men have shown" with their belonging "to the most elevated human civilization." He rejected immediately the "noble savage" answer, which looks to man as "good and noble from his birth" as "not worth taking into consideration." But he began to refine the differentiation between the erotic drives and the "egoistic and cruel drives, condemned by society." The ego drives, which in his earlier view served the instinct of self preservation and the will to power, now became the cruel, the bad drives which society does not allow. Moreover Freud insists that the combined action of the erotic drives with social education produced a kind of biological transformation of the human drives. "Today's men come into the world with a tendency or disposition, to transform the egotistic drives into social ones: soft stimuli (from the education) are now sufficient to make this sort of hereditary organization realizing such a changement."[5]

In this way Freud averted suspicion that the brutal behavior of men in war demonstrated that cultural development, or the civilization process, was an intellectual illusion. He preferred to believe that this deep violence reflected the difficult and painful process of transforming the instincts, which not everyone is able to do. There are men, he said, who are biologically civilized, and men who are not. "You and me," writes Freud to Einstein, "pacifists we are, since our organic nature wills us thus to be... With pacifists like us, the refusal of war is not merely an intellectual and affective repulsion, but a constitutional intolerance...in its most drastic form."[6]

But "organic nature" is not the same for everybody. Not everyone has come to "the strengthening of the intellect, which tends to master our instinctive life," and to the "introversion of the aggressive impulse, with all its consequent benefits and perils." The road was thus open to the later Freud: the Educator, the Philosopher, the Moral Teacher. The dark, which in the infancy of psychoanalysis was nowhere and everywhere, now, in its adult age, has a specific place: with the cruel egoistic drives opposing the good ones of Eros, and contrasted by Society. So light finds its stable place with love and civilized community. No matter if, in everyone's experience, Eros and Thanatos, love and aggression, are profoundly mixed, as they are in war. Not so in later Freud. From the one side is nice Eros, light, enlightenment, education, drives biologically transformed; from the other, Thanatos, archaism, war, egoism, darkness.

So the "dark side" began to act from the beginning of psychoanalytic history. Indeed Freud did not listen too much to the arguments of Lou Andreas Salome, who wrote to him, "I feel inside of me that those more primitive attitudes are not only more archaic, but also the expression of truths which our too civilized Ego at the end rejected."[7] Then psychoanalysis began to mix Freud's declared therapeutic nature with an unofficial educational attitude, and a confusing anthropology. All that led to an undeclared distinction between the good patient, "biologically transformed" in his drives, and the bad one, the archaic, the villain. The "noble civilized" neurotic, the welcomed patient of the enlightened science of the unconscious, is pushed back into the dark, into the multidimensional human being, the legitimate citizen of the entire history of the human psyche, and not only of her momentary, rational last page.

But the dark side of psychoanalysis is not only made by Freud's faith in the enlightenment and his historical connection and faith in light. All along the analytical relation, the search for light, clarity, and respectability, result in the casting of a dark taste on the genuineness of the analytical relationship.

Let us consider the public persona of the founders of the analytical movement. In the beginning, Freud, Jung, as well as many of their followers, were physicians, respected clinicians with a promising future, who chose to risk their success and social position in order to follow their interest in the ambiguous and questionable field of the unconscious. From a Persona point of view, they had everything to lose, and not much to win in this quest. Furthermore the entry into the unconscious meant for them personally, an honest and hard confrontation with their own drives, inhibitions, a risk of their mental equilibrium. Freud had doubts about his own homosexuality,[8] and Jung lived, for a time, in fear of going mad. Open-mindedness toward these disquieting questions on the part of the founders fueled the early psychoanalytic movement with enormous energy and courage, the indispensable qualities necessary to face the darkness of the unconscious.

The situation today is quite different. To choose a psychoanalytic or psychotherapeutic profession is relatively easy. Today nobody risks his reputation in the treatment of the unconscious, as the field is widely acknowledged. Unfortunately, the public recognition of this is comfortable but does not encourage fruitful developments in the field. Particularly when it deals with the darkness, this official recognition and appreciation of the analyst's work has also led to a vanishing of the analyst's openness to look at himself as an ill person, where the ability to cure was based on personal knowledge and an experience with his own illness. The Persona of the early analyst was more akin to that of a Shaman than a medical doctor. Whereas today's image is more commonly that of an expert, a healthy clinician sitting in a chair placed very far from the Acheronte's *"unheimlich"* mud, who liberally accepts to take care of the unfortunate patient.

The darkness of the older style of analysis, which was shared in a painful and difficult path to an only partially happy exit, has been broken by a ray of light that shines also because of the modern analyst's membership in a professional therapeutic organization. Where the founders of the psychoanalytic movement were ambiguous and questionable by definition and carried this burden all their lives, today's analysts are recognized by professional organizations as the "right men," bravely opposing the "bad," the dark, the illnesses of the pathological patient. Positive as this recognition may be as a sign of the growing awareness of the need to treat unconscious contents, that official light breaks the effective tone of the relationship in an analytical setting. Opening the ambiguous analytical relation to the "clarity" of this recognized therapeutic scene, the new analyst's persona makes a tremendous contribution to the development of psychoanalysis' dark contents. This "clarity," this "goodness" itself produces a shadow, a dark.

Another aspect of the dark side of psychoanalysis relates to the operation of the power complex. If, as Freud said and Jung supported, the will to power is an instinct of the Ego,[9] how can the analyst leave it outside of the analytical setting? If we assume that the analyst cares about the analysand, caring can only be guaranteed by keeping alive the awareness that on a moral level the analytical couple is fundamentally equal, the same for both. Both are human beings crossing the difficult situation of the dark, the "*mal de vivre*" and the illness that takes form in it. When the patient is confronted with his shadow, the analyst has to do so too. But the analyst cannot deal with his own shadow moving from a solar and healthy position.

Saint Paul's cry, "Who's the sinner, that I don't match?" should be clearly impressed in the conscience of every analyst. The choice of this attitude, the only one practicable in dealing with the shadow, represented a major change in psychoanalytic philosophy at the beginning of Jung's school of analytical psychology. Philosopher Pier Aldo Rovatti describes it this way:

> …that led the active individual subject (without shadow) into a paradoxical passivity… To recognize the shadow as such means to stop the process of enlightenment of the consciousness activated in this same process. Recognizing the shadow means to realize it. Jung perfectly knows that a recognized shadow is not a light cast on a shadowy area.[10]

To live the shadow in order to transform it, no spot of external light is allowed. If the analyst thinks that it is with his light that the analysand's shadow is penetrated, he assumes a destructive phallic attitude that will cause the shadow to disappear and make any transformation impossible. If the moral level of the two is different: that there is a superior owner of the light, and an inferior wanderer in the shadow; then the will to power intervenes with its characteristic attitude of competition, fight, victory and defeat; and the situation between the two can change, in a way that can become very dangerous. With the analyst reserving for himself the will to power position, the analysand is denied an honest confrontation with his own shadow, which contains his own instincts, drives, their repression and their longing for realization. In surrendering to the will to power the analytical couple reproduces the usual conflict appearing in the individual where the ego ignores recognition of other instincts, especially those relating to sex. For Jung, as well as Freud:

> Human nature bears the burden of a terrible and unending conflict between the principle of the ego and the principle of instinct: the ego all barriers and restraint, instinct limitless, and both principles of equal might.[11]

In speaking about Nietzsche, Jung stresses that philosopher's life was officially devoted to instinct, but was in fact spent in a sort of possession by the opposed drive—the will to power;[12] that in his conflict with Wagner, whom "embodies that other elementary urge," the sexual instinct, Nietzsche was not in fact acting out the sexual instinct, rather the opposed will to power. How often in analysis, officially addressing sex, the instincts and their repression, is the analytical couple unconsciously celebrating other mysteries which are devoted to the *daimon*—will to power, to the magnitude of the ego, the analysand's ego, the analyst's ego, or both? How often, instead of confronting the real Shadow, strongly occupied with the will of power, the analysis is possessed from the unconscious by it, and runs after a false erotic Shadow, strengthened more and more by the force of the only God of the analytic couple? The will to power complex maneuvers the analytical couple from the Shadow of both, pushing them to run after an imaginary "erotic" Shadow, while the unconscious is fully occupied by the contents of the will to power, that are never recognized because both have a defensive attitude toward this material and want to keep it that way. All that denying in the analytical relation, as in daily life, of our neglected Eros, while paying tribute to it in the form of large intellectual homages?

When the analysis slides into a will power mode it emits an heroic atmosphere, which sooner or later will lead to a ruinous fall.[13] The analysand happily projects on to the analyst one image or another of the Hero: the Guru, the Wise Man, the Master, the Warrior. Is this not exactly what the analyst unconsciously wants in his drive to submit the analysand? But acquiring this heroic halo has a price, indeed quite costly. The analysand may become heavily dependent on the Great Analyst. As Mario Jacoby says of this situation, "The analyst is elevated to the rank of an infallible teacher of wisdom, whereby an unconscious fusion with the idealized self-object takes place."[14] Again, "This allows the individual concerned to avoid a confrontation with himself while remaining convinced that he is exploring his own depth. Jung himself spoke in a drastic manner of the dangers inherent to inflationary 'disciple fantasies,' in which one modestly sits at the 'Master's' feet and guards having ideas of one's own. Mental laziness becomes a virtue; one can at least bask in a sun of a semi-divine being."[15]

Avoiding this danger is not only a matter of controlling a more or less conscious will to power, it also involves another aspect of the darkness of analysis, or the labor of seeing through fascination itself. Unconscious contents flowing from the analysand's psyche into the analytical setting, and represented to him in the voice of the analyst, contain a rich and mysterious charm, which is difficult to resist. "Looking into the water one sees, it's true, one's own image," Jung said. "But very soon, behind it, living beings will emerge. Probably fish. Sometimes an undine, half human, gets tangled into the fisherman's net. Undines are charming beings."[16] And quoting Goethe, "Half way she pulled, half way he sank and nobody saw him anymore." This risk is high in any treatment of the unconscious. The analytical relation is always on the border of an abyss where the moral integrity of the analytical couple (but particularly that of the analyst), may collapse and vanish.

From one side the unconscious contents, enormously wider and richer than that of consciousness, exercise a powerful attraction on the analyst's libido, acting far from the ego's control. From the other side the analyst's consciousness may see in those strange and charming images a chance to compensate for the daily landscape, with its boredom and mediocrity, in this case the poison of the unconscious, which should act as a homeopathic remedy for the analysand, becomes the beloved drug of the analyst, who slips into addiction. He needs, and loves, the poison which the analysand's unconscious is slowly secreting. As an addict, the analyst is no longer a therapist; he cannot cure.

This abyssal vertigo is always near, and the analyst must control it without rest; a risk of his very life. The risk can't be avoided. The analyst, it's true, may choose not to listen erotically to the analysand's song, but that would lead the analysis to a dead point. For if he wants to save a therapeutic effectiveness he's forbidden to assume the position of the teacher, the master, the medical doctor. These are all very respectable figures that can in no way help the analysand transform his darkness, because they do not love the darkness and keep distance from it, relying on their respective tools—pedagogy, faith, science—to promote an attitude of dry, sterile power.

The image of Odysseus, bound, listening to the Siren's song, represents the core of this problem. Who makes the seaman-analysand listen to the Siren's song? The analyst, of course. But how to remain the one who makes the analysand listen to the Siren's song, without becoming the singing Siren? The question is not an odd one, nor is it easy to answer. The analyst has to remain open to the charm of the analysand's unconscious, but "bound" with the strong ropes of ethical obligation, in order to lead the analysand out of those dangerous waters. Only thus may he help the other person constellate the Odysseus archetype, the character in a man who dares to listen to the unconscious, while forbidding himself to be taken in by it.

For the analyst to renounce being an irresistible Siren is not an easy choice. But if the analysand does not perceive clearly, at a deep level, the difference between the analyst who makes possible the listening to the Siren's song, and the Siren singing, he will strongly resist the analysis. After all it would be a sane reaction, for his own psychic survival. The Odysseus-analysand may limit his precaution to asking the sailors to bind him to the mast, or prefer to stuff his ears with wax, to hear nothing and take no risk. Or decide to get off so dangerous a boat and break the analysis altogether. It is the analyst's responsibility to avoid confusing the relationship with the therapist with the relationship to the Siren. If the analyst renounces the will to power and the narcissistic dream of becoming the analysand's most precious relation, the analysand can be healed by crossing the unconscious, without falling into a dark possession by the analyst.

The analyst should renounce possession of the unconsciously charming contents of wisdom and seduction that are represented by the Sirens, that appear on the surface, through his accurate work, and his passion for the analysand. He should likewise refuse to be possessed by those same charming creatures that move and act under his own eyes, specially for him. The first refusal bleeds his narcissism. The second refusal bleeds his heart and his sex. For this is precisely the transference problem. It is comparatively easy to forgo falling in love with one's own mother, or daughter (as acted out by the female analysand). It is much more difficult not to oppose the powerful, charming contents of the collective unconscious, now appearing and acting just in front of his arm chair.

The analyst has to put away a *mana,* the charming energy ready-made, which the analysand freely attributes to him. To do this he must accept to deceive the analysand, who wants to make grandiose the analyst's image. For grandiosity feeds on his own narcissism; the analysand of a grandiose analyst is himself grandiose. Grandiosity feeds on his own sadism; it will come time for the analysand to destroy the grandiose image of the analyst which has become so embarrassingly great. This same psychological attitude leads the desperate masses of a totalitarian political system first to enjoy themselves in erecting magnificent statues to the Tyrant, then later to break them into dust with a vicious satisfaction.

The analyst has to resist his own obvious narcissism and natural will to power which is allied for opposite purposes to the narcissism and will to power of the analysand. The analyst is tempted to take possession of Siren's song to assert himself, and the analysand wants him to take possession of it in order to destroy him and his analysis. To avoid this ruinous issue the analyst should submit himself to the less grandiose role of the director of the play, or better, of the owner of Odysseus' ship. A shipowner is a character all but grandiose, who usually stays in a dusty office (for example the dark *"scagni"* of Genoa's harbor), keeping the analysand's time-contract, a mercenary relation not entirely destitute of erotic content. It is certainly more difficult to maintain a role half way between the shipowner and the prostitute (which is the archetype of the analyst, according to Ricardo Musatti), than it is to accept being a beautiful, irresistible Siren. But this middle role has to be played to avoid slipping into the dark side.

The analyst who is drawn to the high tones of the Siren's song, who makes a show of their profound wisdom as if it were his own, and who sings of his desire to possess the other as a siren does, is imprisoned by the dark side of the analytical relation. It would be very difficult for his Odysseus not to run into the rocks awaiting the journey. On the other hand, the analyst who accepts being a modest shipowner, financially interested in a good end to the journey, will absorb all the rage of the analysand's frustrated narcissism. The analysand will not easily forgive the analyst's unassuming common sense. The analyst's cautious refusal to sing the Siren's melody will be interpreted as bourgeoisie cowardice. And the analyst's unwillingness to accept the Siren's song as the soundtrack of the analytical relationship, will be attributed to his coldness, lack of imagination, and a tendency to be formal.

The analyst should accept, humbly, those painful acknowledgments, which are the unavoidable price of his moral obligation not to play suggestion's card, and to frustrate the temptation to exert his will to power in the analytical relationship. The analytical encounter (as Ricardo Musatti obstinately repeats) is a "trivial" one, in the etymological sense that it happens at a place the old Latins called a *trivium*, a place where one road opens in multiple directions, and where the prostitute waits, at night, offering herself to move the erotic imagination of the wanderer. In this half light, the two will meet, and unite under the protection of the Gods of relation, desire, and freedom. The wanderer will pay and go, now in touch with his deep instinctual energy, with a sense of physical and spiritual energy engraved in it. Every attempt to refuse the "trivial" light of this encounter in favor of a more shining position, will activate the dark side of the analysis, where the charming power of the analyst will cause the death of the wanderer's soul.

If the individuation process has the goal "to become what you are," all of the analyst's attempts to avoid the darkness, either the analysand's or his own, to keep some light for himself, will result in a diversion from the true goal of the process. The analysand will not become who he is, but what the analyst wants he should be, to gratify his own narcissism and will to power. In this way the analytical couple will reach not the analysand's individuation, but a new edition of an old false self (of the analysand, of the analyst, or both), which will be stronger and somehow renewed from an enriching research into unconscious depth.

The dark side of psychoanalysis is under-girded by a specific method of forming, or training the analyst. This method is later adopted by him and perpetuated in the technique of working with the unconscious contents of his analysands. I call this method "literalism."

By "literalism" I mean the way the analyst explains what is happening in the scene to be analyzed: what is being said, what is being acted, who is acting, in the belief that everything may be, has to be interpreted. Just as he was trained to do in supervisory sessions. As French philosopher Gilles Deleuze says, "interpretation is the religious devotion of modernity; the devotion to rationality." This faith in rationality leads the analytic process through a sequence of intellectual concepts on which the interpretation is based. What is literal in this process is the application of psychological meaning to words and gestures, interpreted with the help of intellectual concepts, but without being connected to the images behind those being analyzed. But it is because of those images, archetypes maneuvering at the back of apparent reality, that the analysand's situation is what it is. Likewise, it is those same images, activated and constellated during the analytical process, that will produce a transformation in the analysand's psyche.

C. G. Jung insists that images are the true language of the unconscious, while emphasizing that rational and intellectual approaches are only of partial and approximate utility in seizing the meaning of their archaic, instinctive and collective contents. The unconscious speaks, he says, "The Anima, the psyche, is a sequence of images."[17] "The so called concept is nothing but a shortened description or definition of psychic facts,"[18] which the psyche expresses directly through images.[19] Images appear in dreams, or in a creative activity like sand play; that's the language of the unconscious.

This vision of unconscious language, made by images, is tied to Jung's belief in the scientific inconsistency of psychology, and in the fanciful pretension of being able to "explain the psyche through the psyche." If then the goal of Jung's "individuation process" is the centering of the personality on the unconscious, and the unconscious expresses itself through images, the training of the analyst will consist in developing a capacity for receiving those images and being empathetic with them. So what is needed is not a reduction of those images to concepts through the rational interpretation of psychic imagery, but the development in the analyst of a large and sensible experience with imaginal knowledge. The consciousness of the analyst should be large enough to consent to the analysand's images, to let them move as they need and represent what they are.

The "good" therapist then will not be the one to understand the intellectual meaning of the images presented by the unconscious, but the one who is able to make them move, to help make them manifest, to realize their action, to activate and pursue their therapeutic destiny, which Freud intuitively understood as the "destiny of the drives" and recognized as the "mythology of psychoanalysis." Thus in Jungian psychology the analyst's technique becomes a "dynamic," an "ethic," or the "imaginal world." That is why in analytical psychology the therapist's formation and training cannot be realized in the same way as anyone else's psychology on the market, where the psyche is explained by the psyche, a notion that gets on Jung's nerves. It is not in reducing images from the unconscious to psychological concepts intellectually made by consciousness that a transformation may take place. It will happen when the therapist recognizes the psychological atmosphere of the unconscious images, and the meaning of their appearance.

A personal opening to the imaginal world is also enhanced by study in the fields of anthropology, history of religion, art, archeology, communications, and sciences where images similar to those arising in the unconscious appear, as happens in biology, physics, mathematics. All the experience of "The Art of Memory" showed through the centuries how intellectual concepts and tools tend to fade the precious contents of psychological and symbolic memories that we are carrying in ourselves. Plato made clear the psychological and moral difference between images and concepts, which later Jung set on the basis for the individuation process, and for his therapeutic technique.

In Plato's *Phaedrus* Socrates tells the story of Toth, one of the most ancient of Egyptian Gods, who was the inventor of numbers, of calculation, astronomy, and the alphabet. He went to King Thamus, insisting on the diffusion of his inventions among all the Egyptians. But the king's reaction to the invention of the alphabet was particularly bitter. He complained that it will generate oblivion in the souls of the people who will learn it. They will cease to exercise their memory, because trusting in writing they will recall facts to their mind no more through the inside of themselves, but through external signs: the letters of the alphabet. You're not offering a true wisdom to your pupils, but only an external appearance. Thus they, thanks to your discovery, will be able to have information about a lot of things without experiencing anything. They'll believe themselves to be profound scholars, without knowing anything. They will be stuffed with opinion, instead of being wise. The opposition here is between knowledge based on concept, or verbal forms made by trained thinking, and knowledge provided from a vision of the archetypes, or primordial images which may be perceived by a soul orientated to interior rather than external signs.

In the medieval art of memory Albertus Magnus explains that

> a) Images constitute an indispensable help for memory's activity. b) A few images help to remember many things. c) Accurate descriptions (*propria*) may give a more precise information on things, but metaphoric images (*methaforica*) move the *anima*.[20]

In other words, metaphoric images are better for psychological memory.

These commentaries by Plato and Albertus Magnus may help clarify what I mean when I call "dark" the intellectual "literalism" of the analytical method of interpretation. "Concepts," "rationality," while pretending to explain, to "enlighten" the images of the unconscious, instead cast them farther away from the psychological sight of the analytical couple, into a dead and motionless darkness.[21] It's the place of the poor Wild Man, Heisen Hans (of the Grimm fairy tale), fixed in the depth of the "pond" that is the unconscious, by the nasty, rationally interpretative attitude of the anti-natural side of Christianity. A long time is needed to take him out from this silent tomb. Great efforts by Robert Bly and others[22] have only had the effect of provoking shy tremors in the powerful giant blocked by *intellectus rigor mortis*.

It is only in accepting the apparent darkness of the images of the unconscious, in accepting to soak in their ambiguous, archaic, imaginal world, in refusing the hurry of rational interpretation and the reduction to *intellectus*, that we can finally hope to reach the internal light and energy of the images, and to allow them to softly enlighten the slender path to individuation. Repeating the metaphor of Jean de la Cruz, "It is only in the dark of the night that we can hope to see the long awaited face of the beloved."[23]

Notes

1   Ernest Jones, *The Life and Work of Sigmund Freud* (New York: Basic Books, 1962).
2   C. G. Jung, "On the Psychology of the Unconscious," in *The Collected Works of C. G. Jung* (hereafter abbreviated as *CW*), (London: Routledge), vol. 7, par. 35.
3   Sigmund Freud, "Drei Abhandlungen zur Sexualtheorie," in *Gesammelte Werke des Sigmund Freud* (hereafter abbreviated as *GW*), vol. 5.
4   Jones, *op. cit.*
5   Freud, "Zeitgemasses uber Krieg und Tod," *GW*, vol. 8.
6   Albert Einstein and Sigmund Freud, *Why War?* (Geneva: League of Nations, 1933).
7   Jones, *op cit*; Ernst Kris, *The Origins of Psychoanalysis: Letters to Wilhelm Fliess, Drafts and Notes, 1887-1902* (London: Imago), 1954.
8   Jung, *Memories, Dreams, Reflections* (hereafter abbreviated as *MDR*), recorded and edited by Aniela Jaffe, translated by R. and C. Winston, (London; Fontana, 1983).
9   Jung, "On the Psychology of the Unconscious," *CW*, vol. 7.
10 P. A. Rovatti, *L'esercizio del silenzio* (Milano: Cortina, 1992).
11 Jung, "On the Psychology of the Unconscious," par. 43.
12 *Ibid.*
13 *Ibid.*
14 Mario Jacoby, *Individuation and Narcissism* (London: Routledge, 1990).
15 Jung, 'The Relations Between the Ego and the Unconscious," *CW* 7, par. 263.
16 Jung, *MDR*.
17 Jung, *La dimensione psichica* (Torino: Boringhieri, 1982), p 143.
18 *Ibid.*
19 Furthermore, as Jung explains in *MDR*, those images protect the individual from the emotional strength of the crude contents of the unconscious.
20 Albertus Magnus, *Opera Omnia*, ed. A. Borgnet (Paris: 1890), p. 251.
21 Here I want to stress the connection between Freudian anthropology and the rational and evolutional views of the Enlightenment and Modernity. While Jung, with his emphasis on images being larger than rational concepts, is already Post-Modern.
22 Robert Bly, *Iron John: A Book About Men* (Reading, Massacheutsetts: Addison Wesley Publishing Co.) ; C. Rise, *Il Maschio Selvatico*, (Como: Red, 1995).
23 G. Della Croce, "Nolte oscura," *Opere* (Rome, Postulazione Generale dei Carmelitani Scalzi, 1979).

CONTRIBUTORS

Claudio Bonvecchio (1947) is a Laureato in Theoretical Philosophy, Extraordinary Professor for Political Philosophy, and Dean of Political Science in Trieste, Italy. He is also the author of numerous books on the subject of myth and symbols in politics. At this time, he is writing on the myth and symbol of the Emperor.

Michiyoshi Hayashi (1937) is Professor at Tokyo Women's Christian University, specializing in depth psychology and its relation to the social sciences. He is also an analyst in private practice. Currently, he is president of the Japanese Association of Jungian Studies and a member of the Association of Comparative Philology. His publications include works on Weberian sociology, Stalinism and Jungian methods and figures in Japanese myth.

Mikiko Ishii is a Professor at Kanagawa University, Yokohama-shi of English Literature. She taught at Cambidge University from 1974 to 1978.

Jay Livernois (1956) is a translator of medieval Italian Poetry and managing editor of Spring Publications. He is currently completing his book on the origins of the Puritan aesthetic.

Claudio Risé (1939) is an analyst in private practice in Milan. He is a member of the board of the International Association for Sandplay Therapy and directs the publication series "Immagini del Profondo" and "Quaderni di Eranos" for *red edizione*, one of Italy's leading psychological publishers. His recent work on male psychology includes *Parsifal* and *The Savage Mask*.

Christa Robinson (1940) is the President of the Eranos Foundation.

Eiji Uehiro (1937) is chairman of the Uehiro Foundation on Ethics and Education at the Practical Ethics Association which is Japan's largest social education organization with a membership of over four million. He is the author of many books on ethical and social issues, including *An Introduction to Practical Ethics* and *The Era of Practical Ethics*.